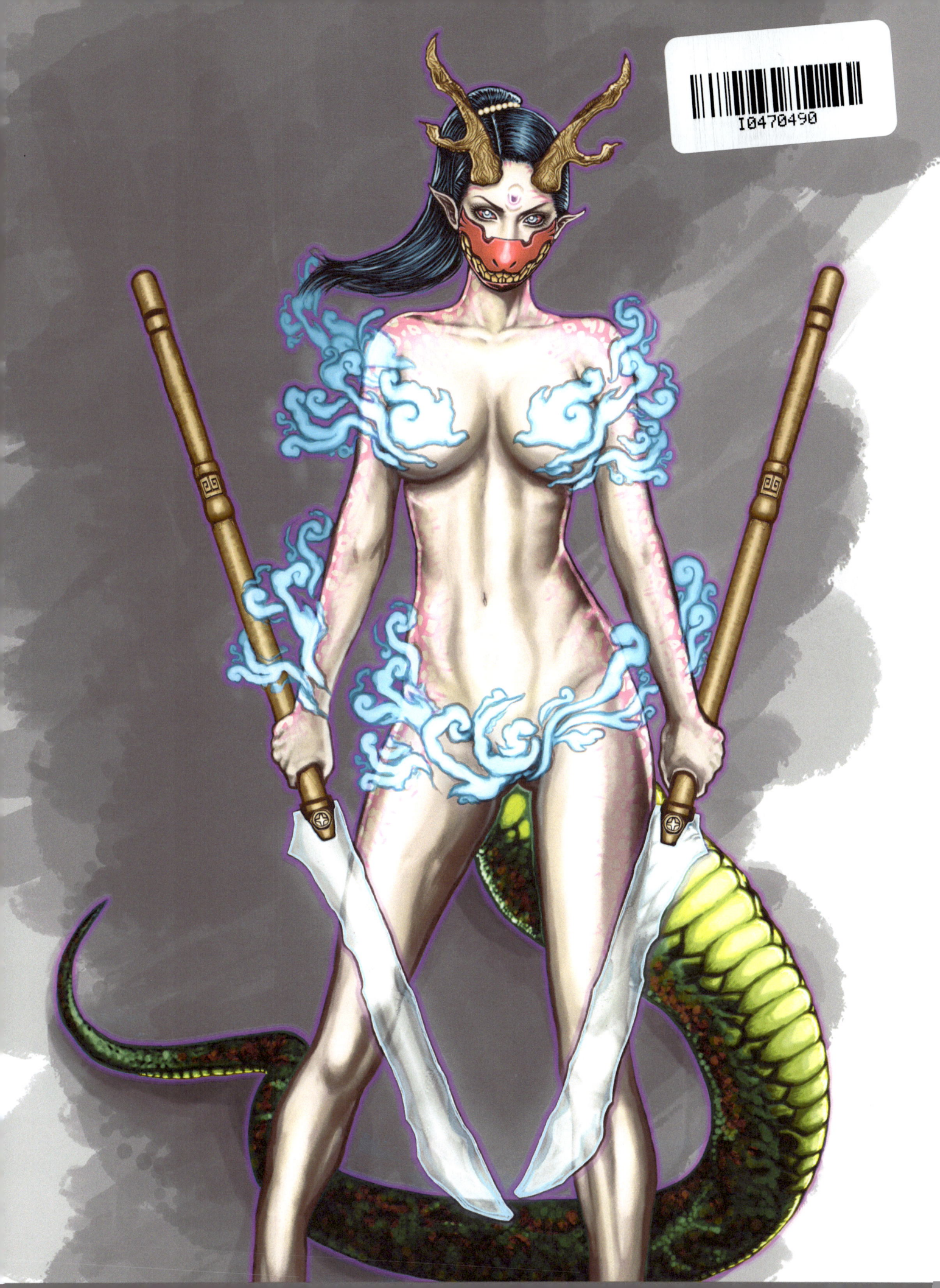

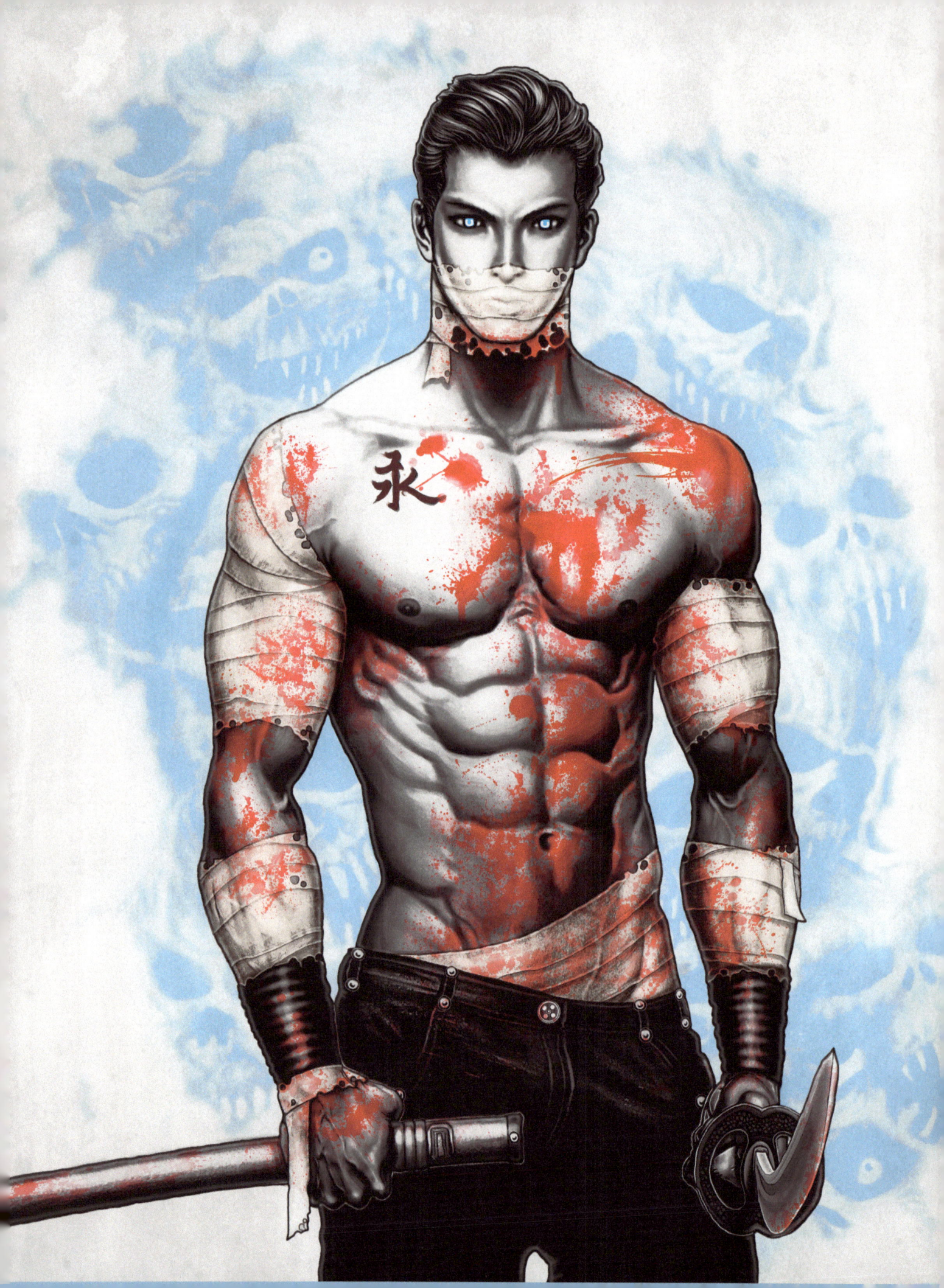

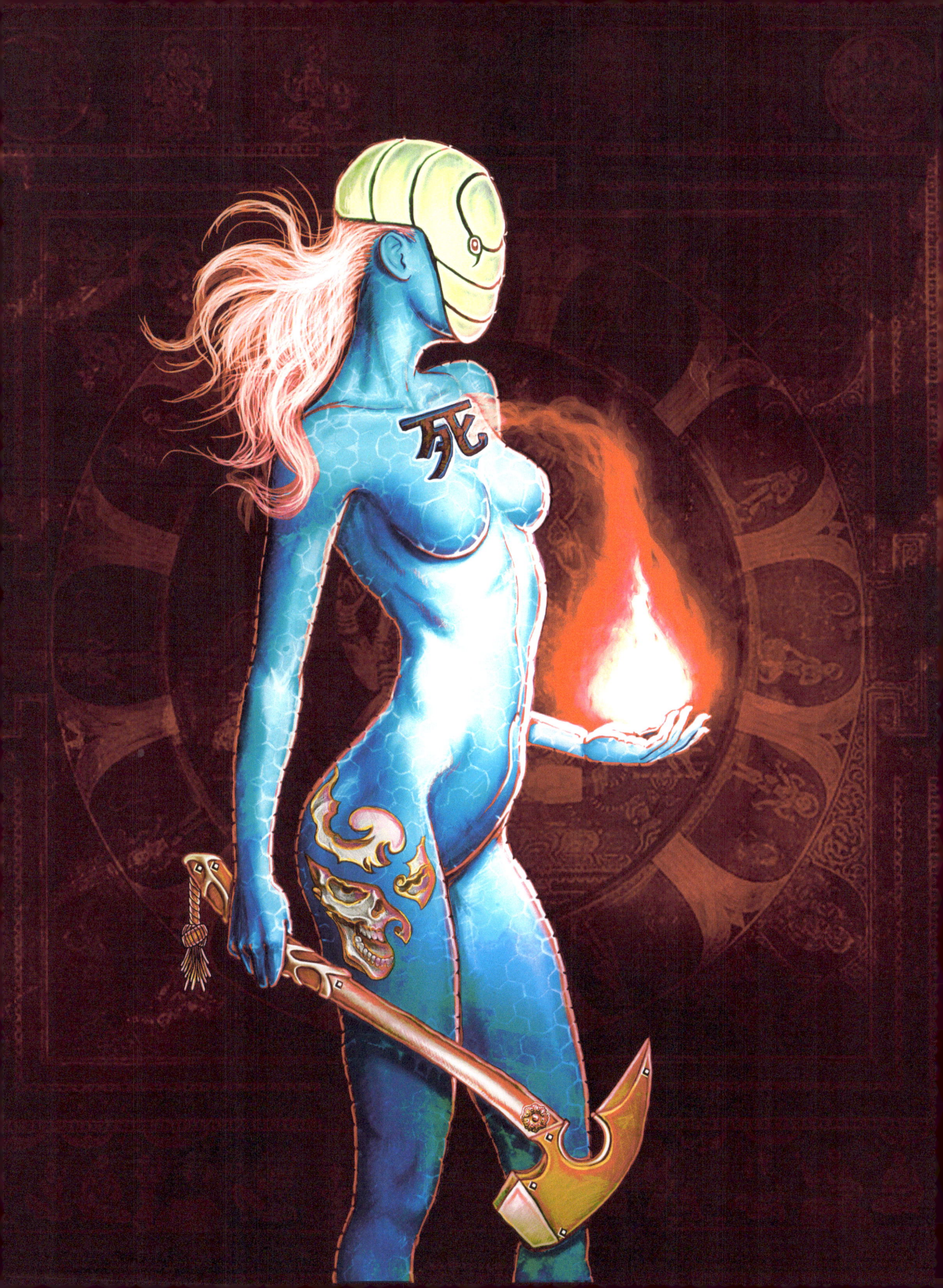

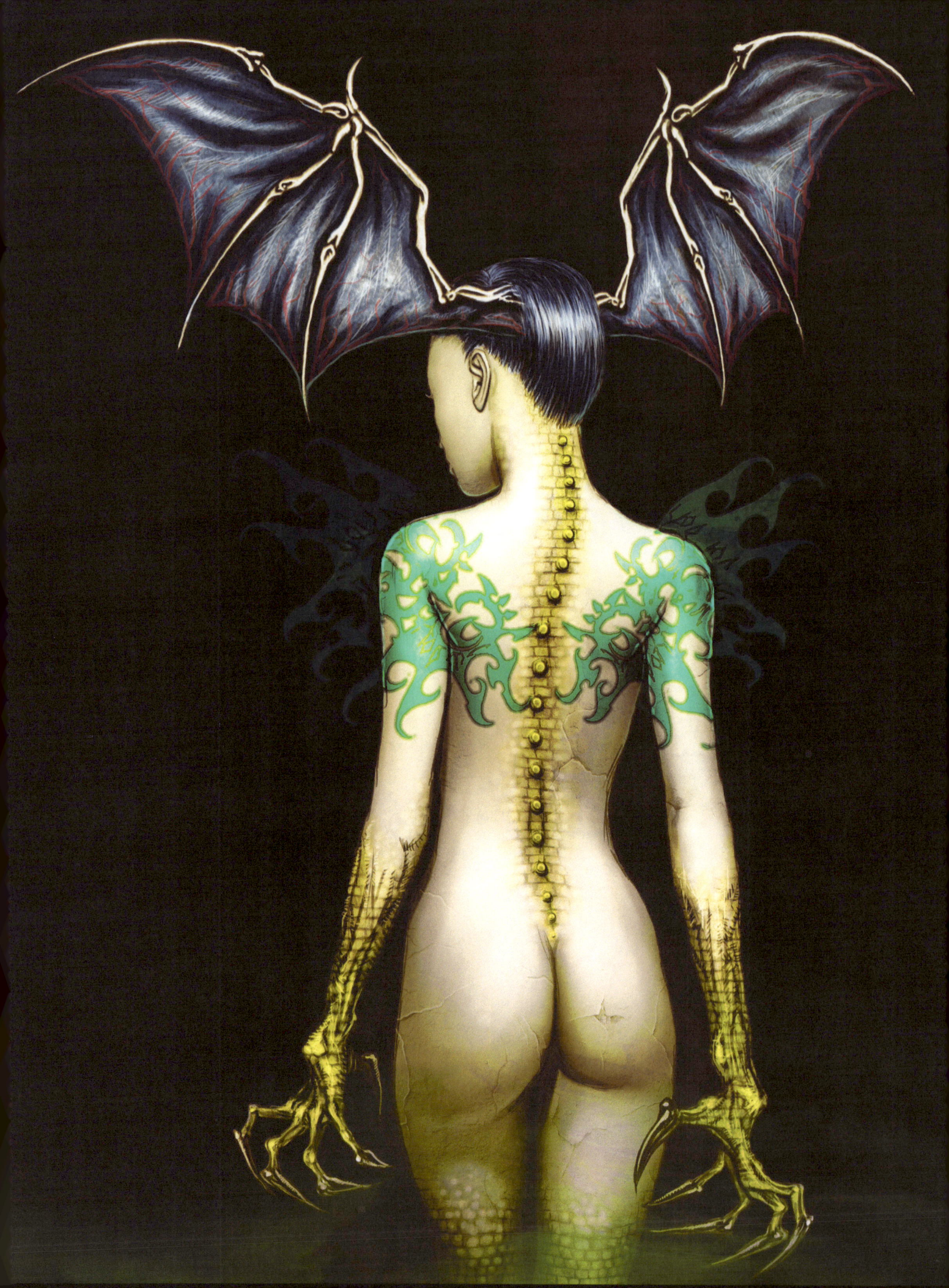

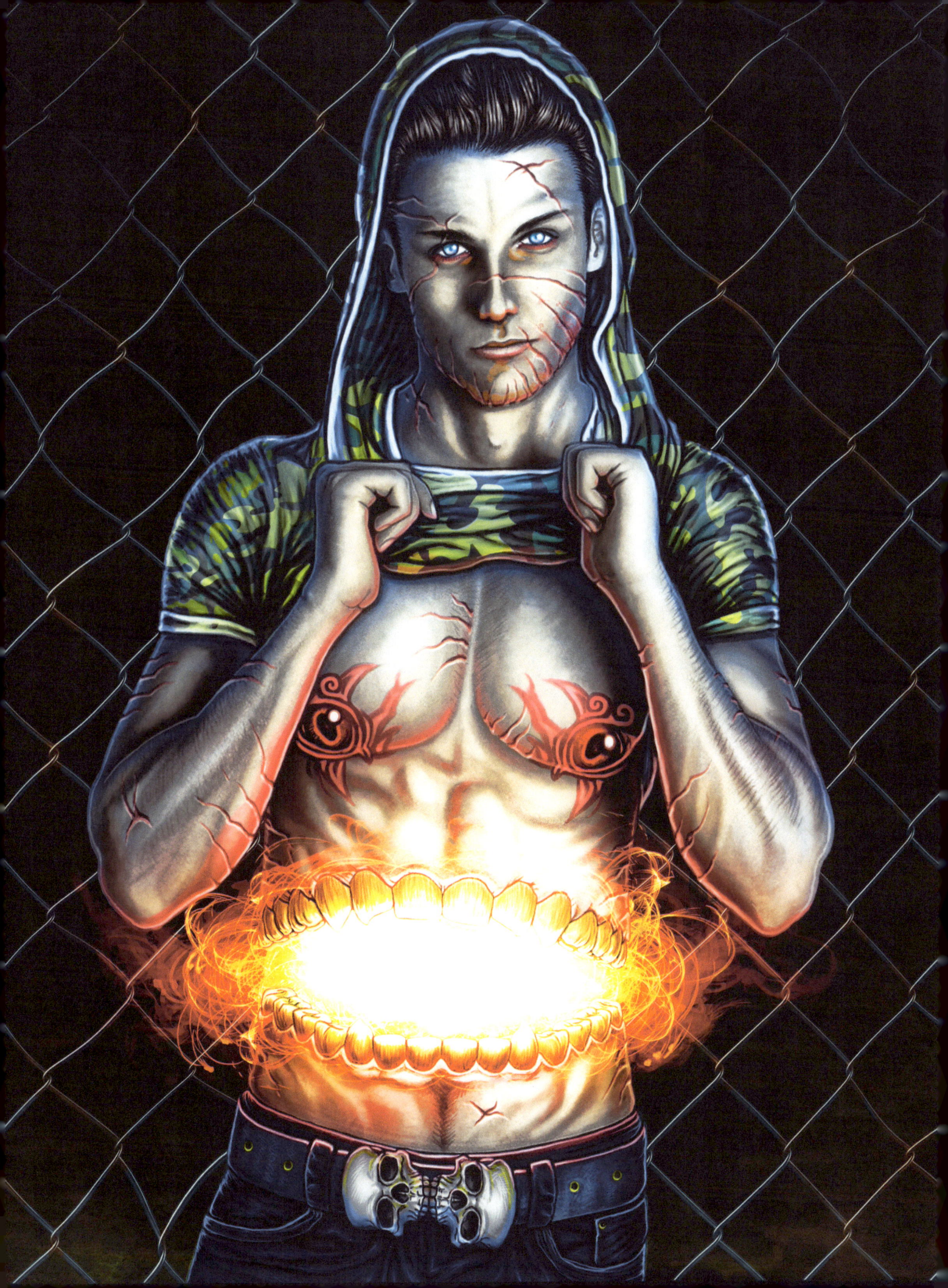

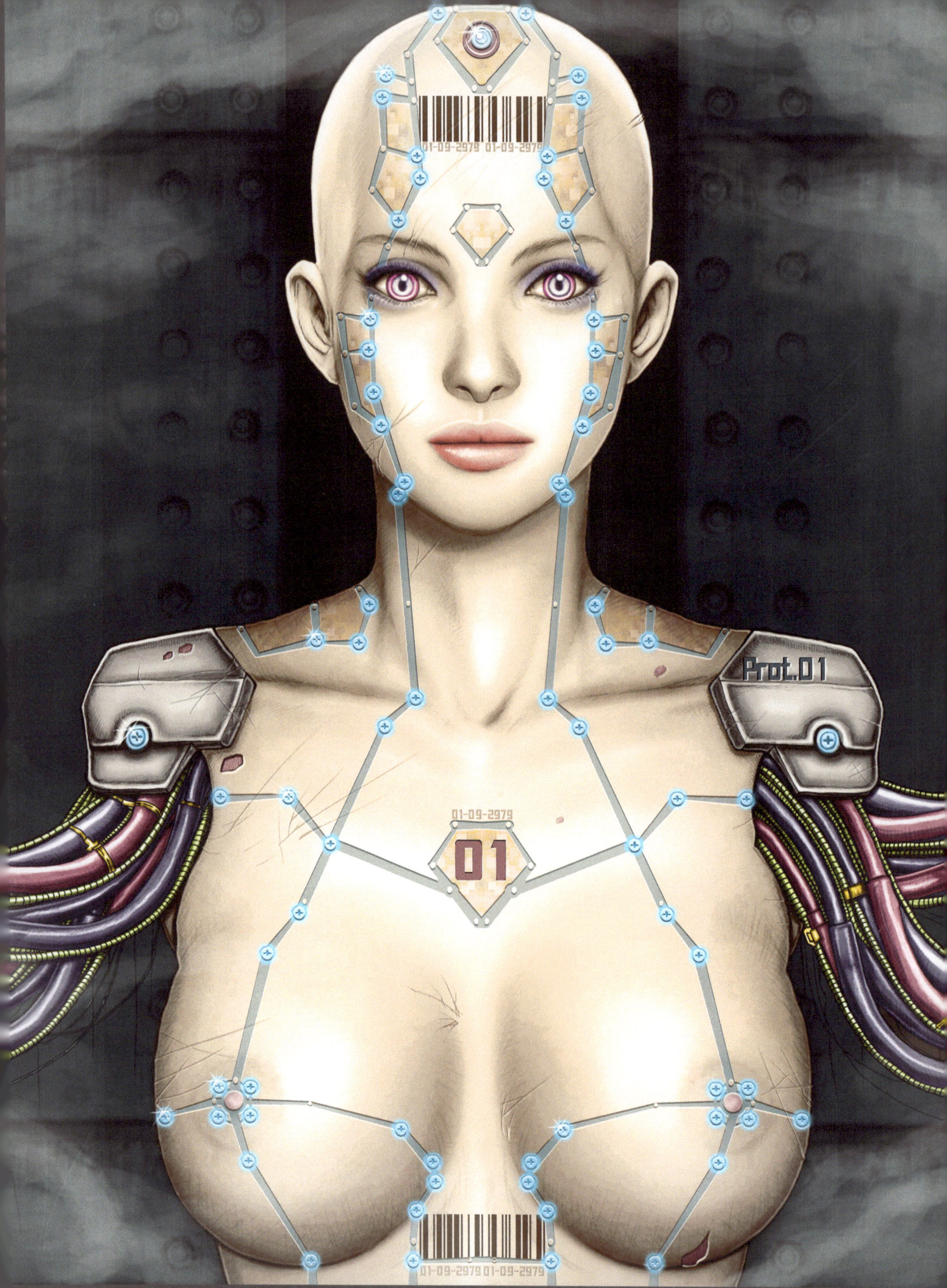

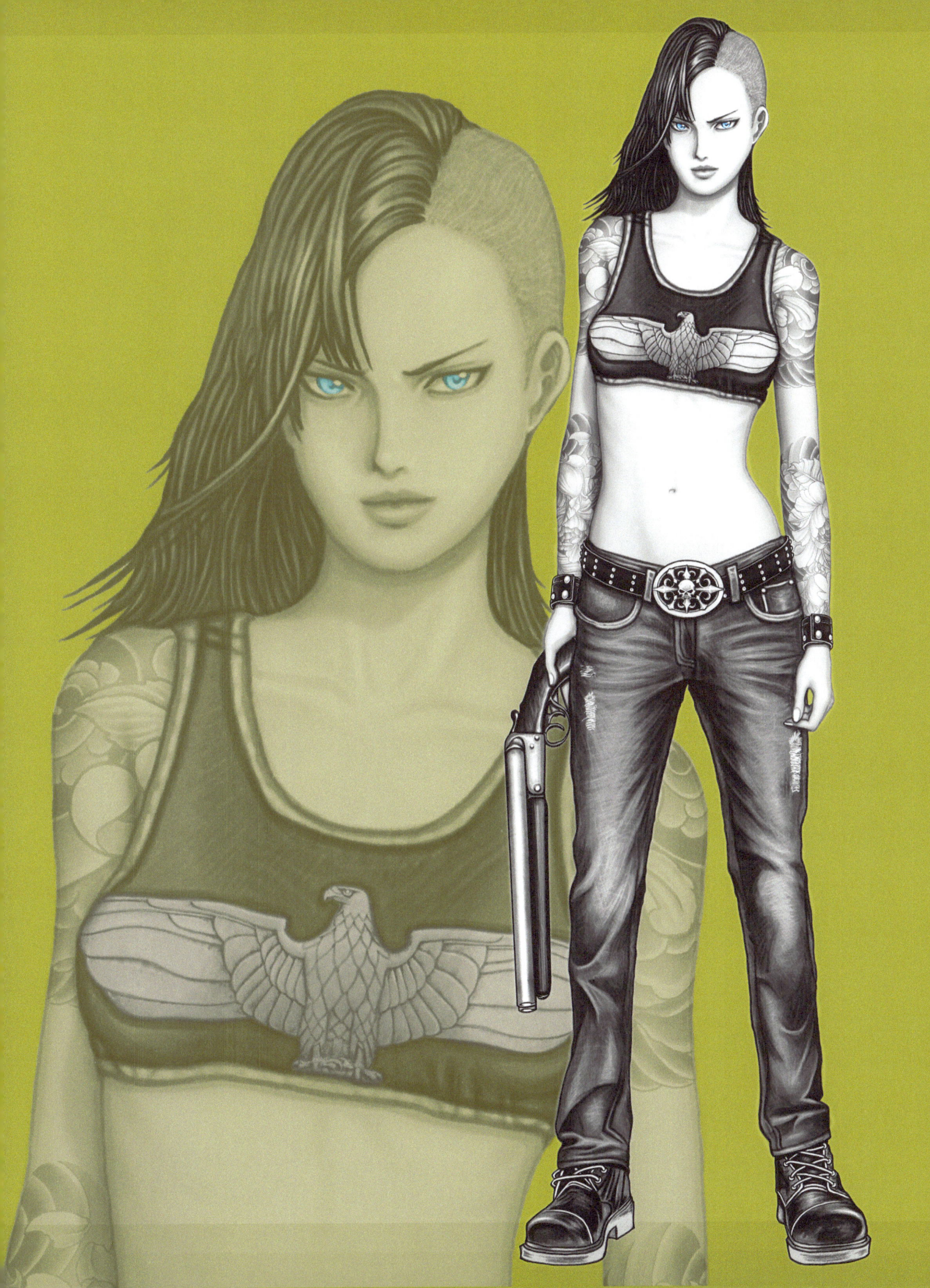

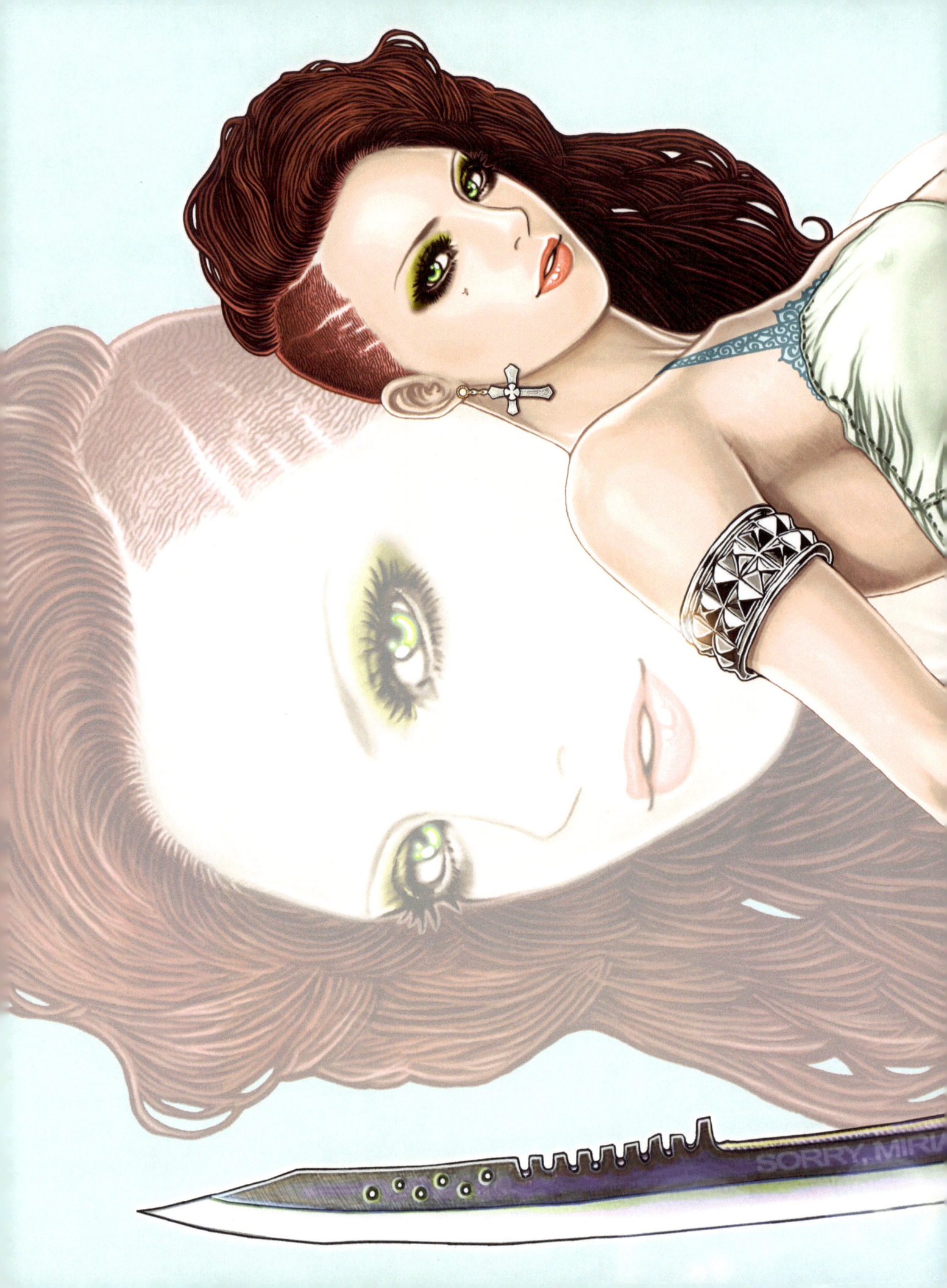

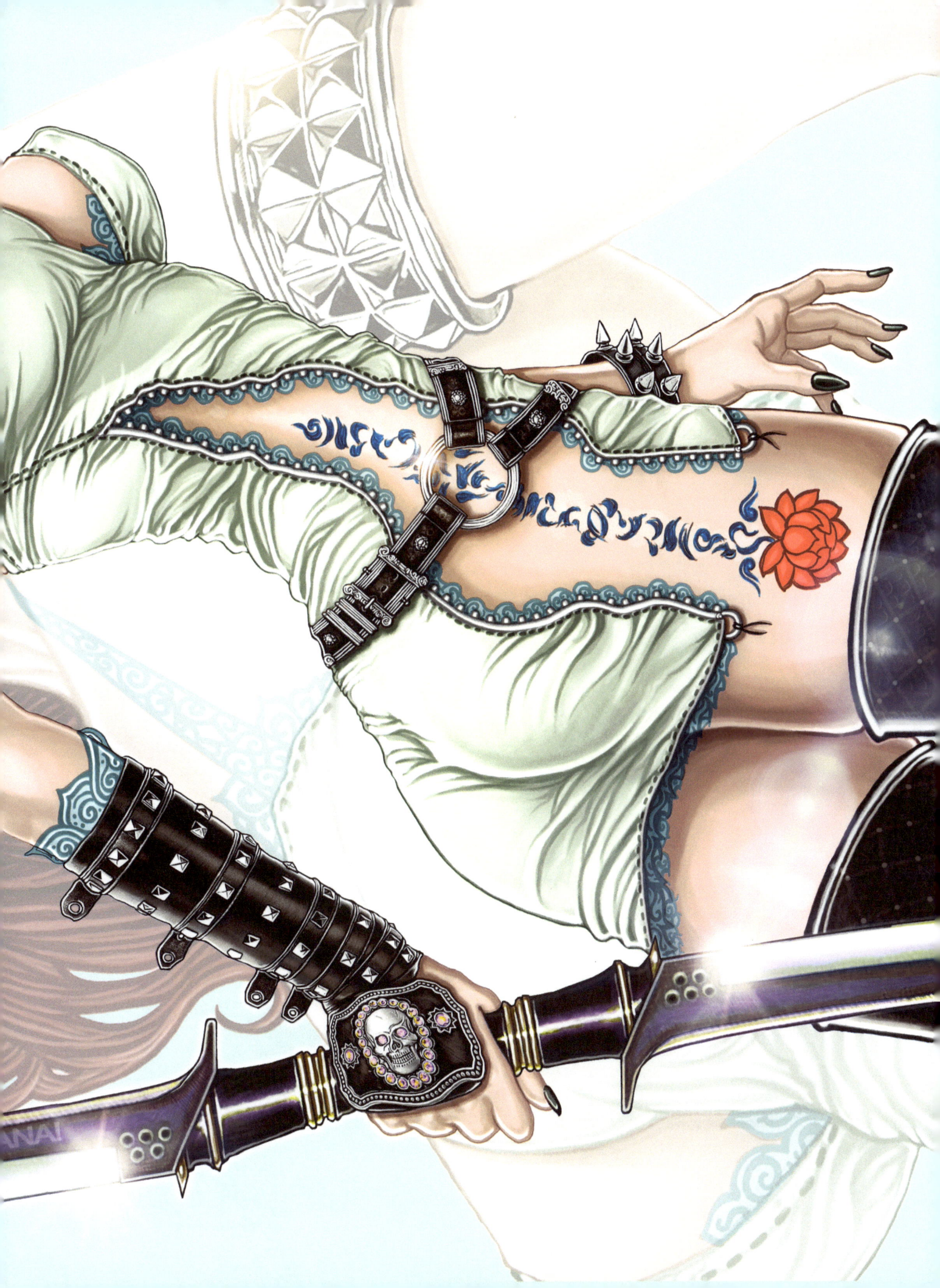

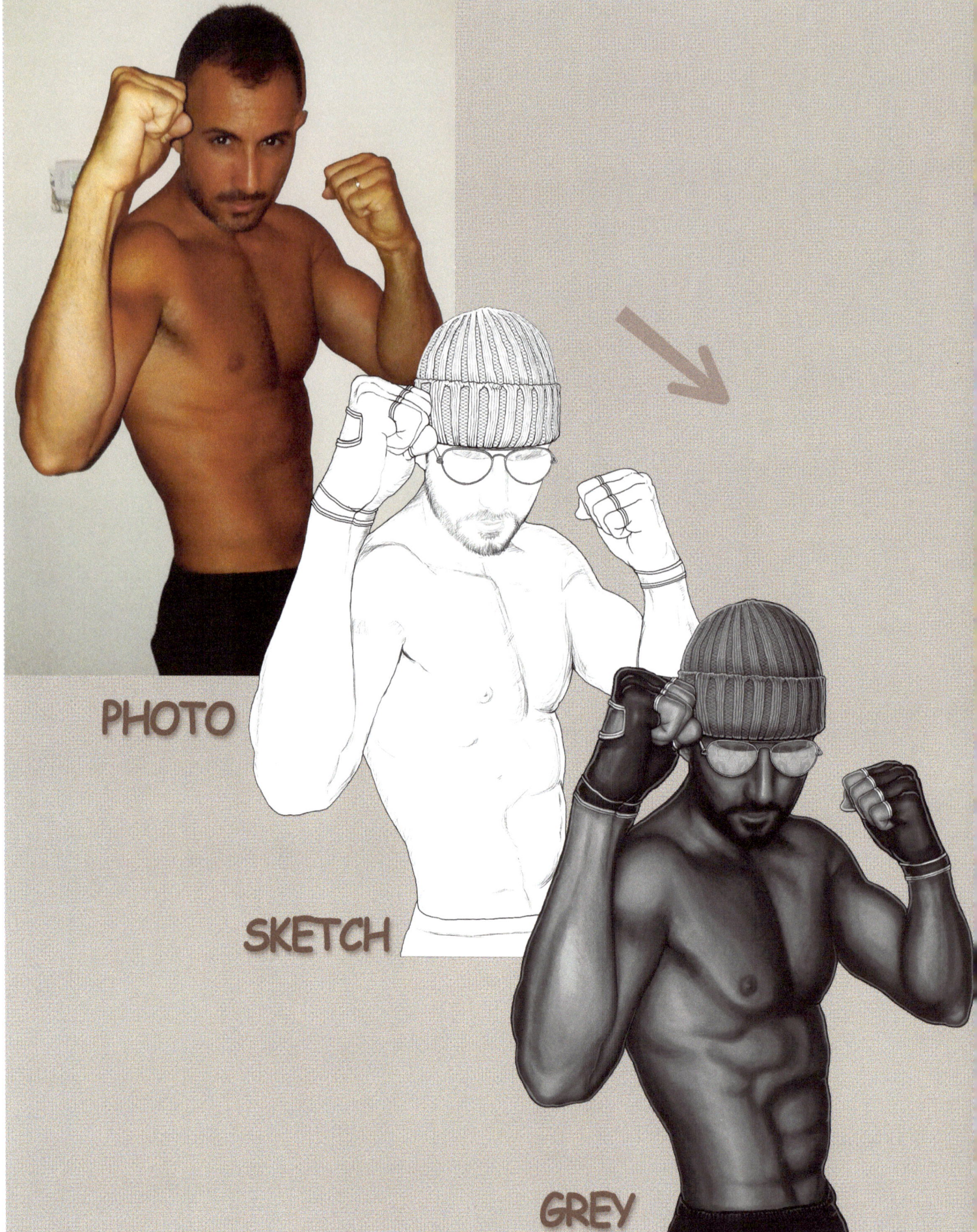

PHOTO

SKETCH

GREY

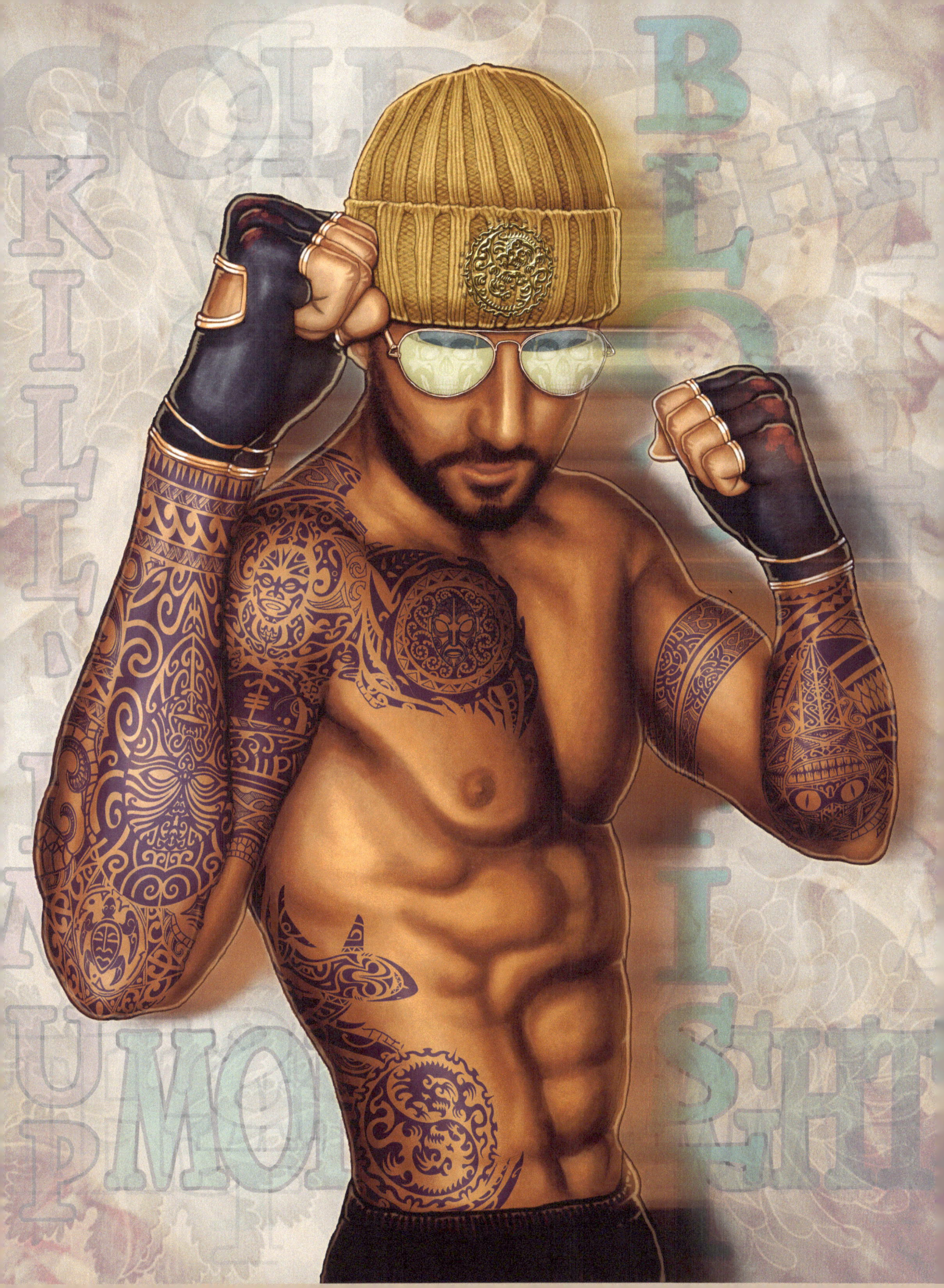

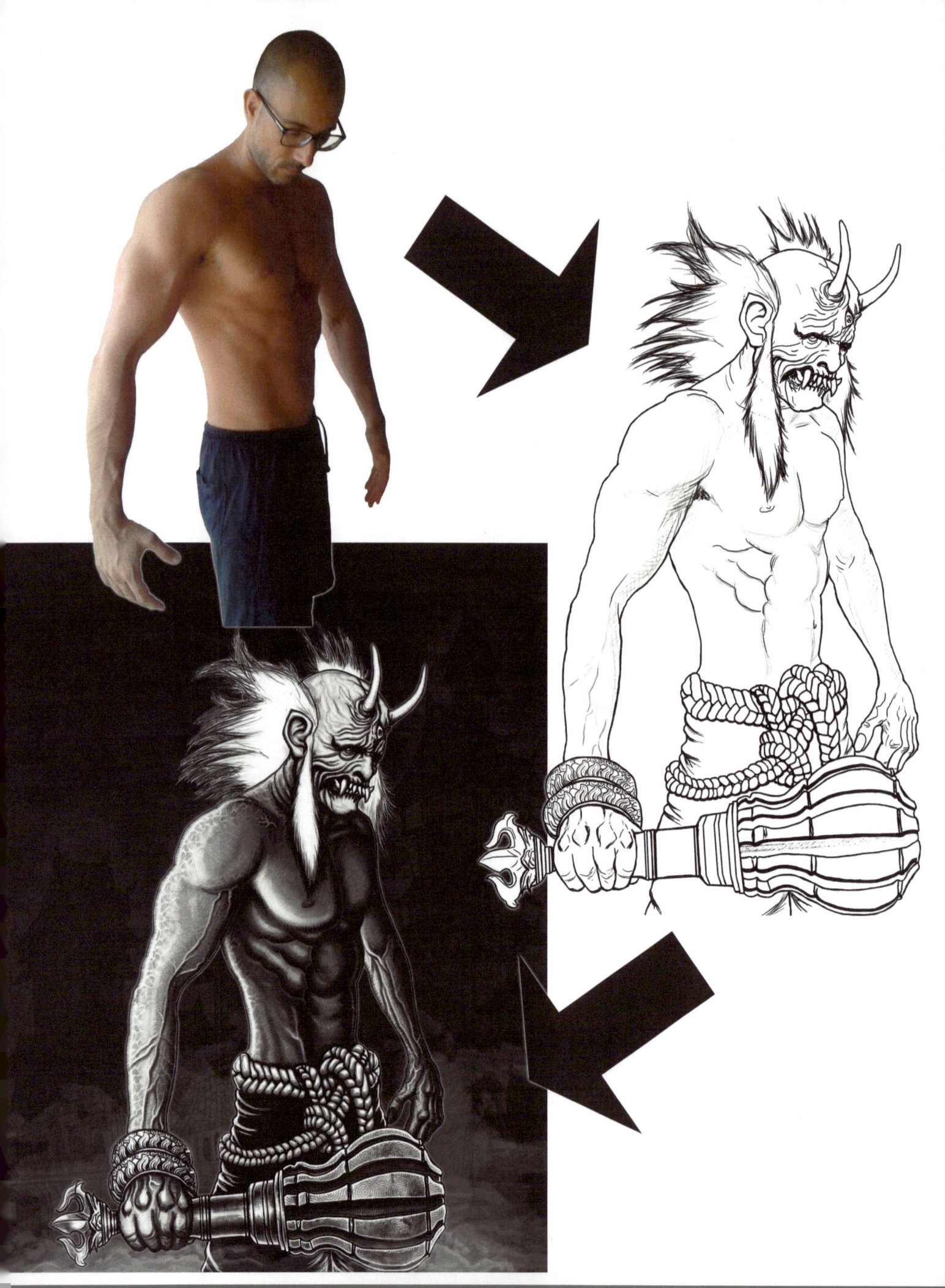

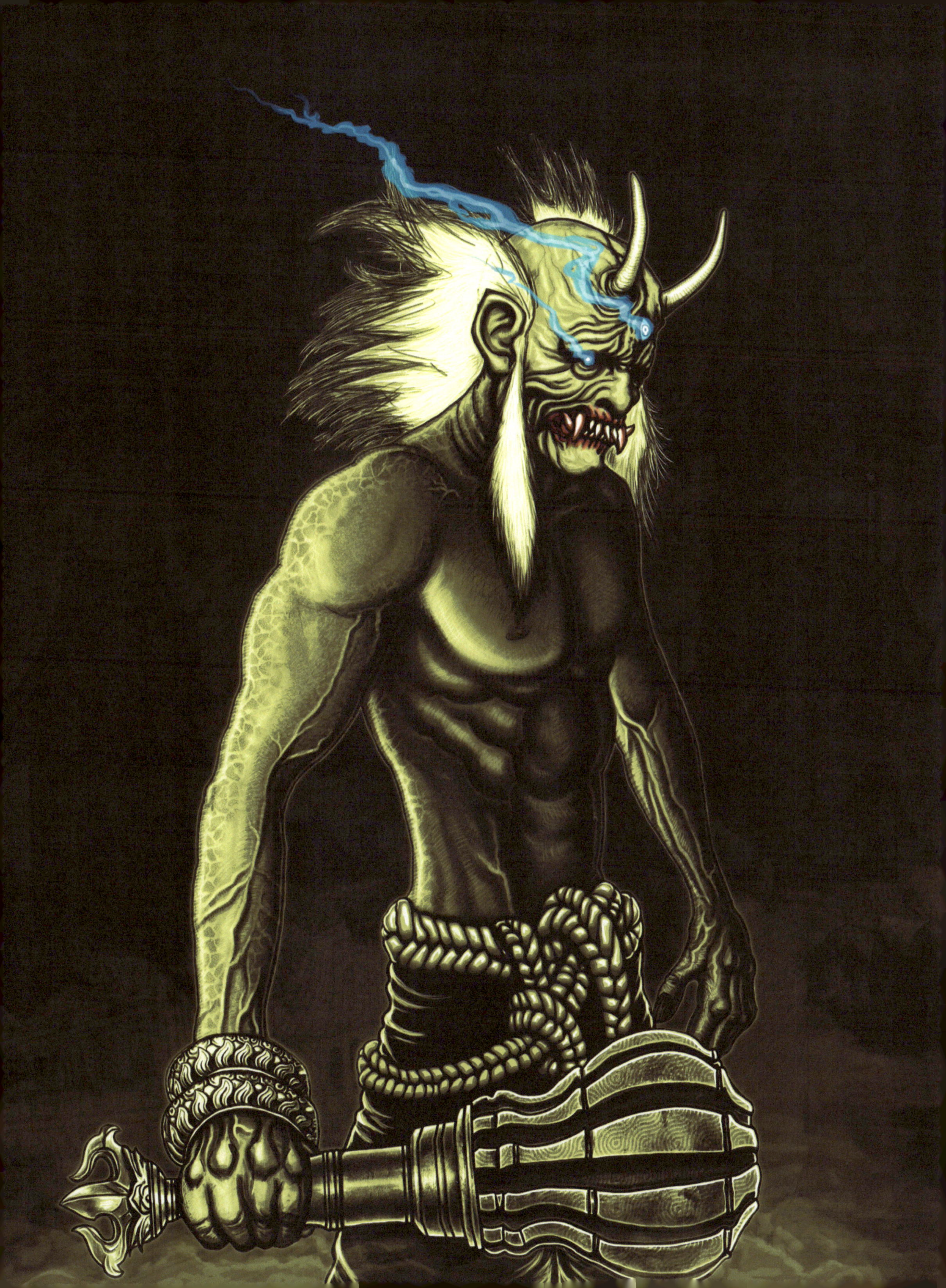

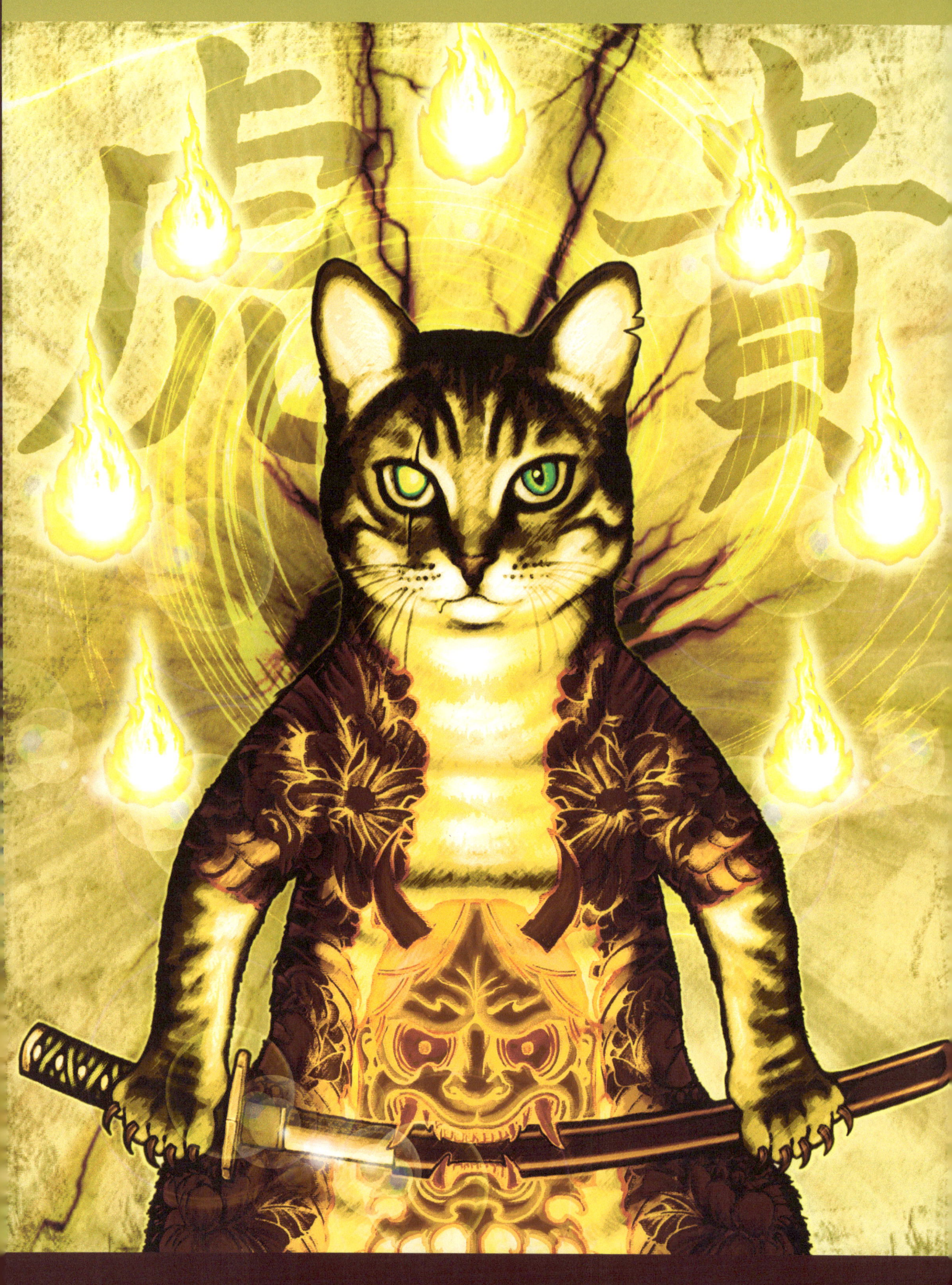

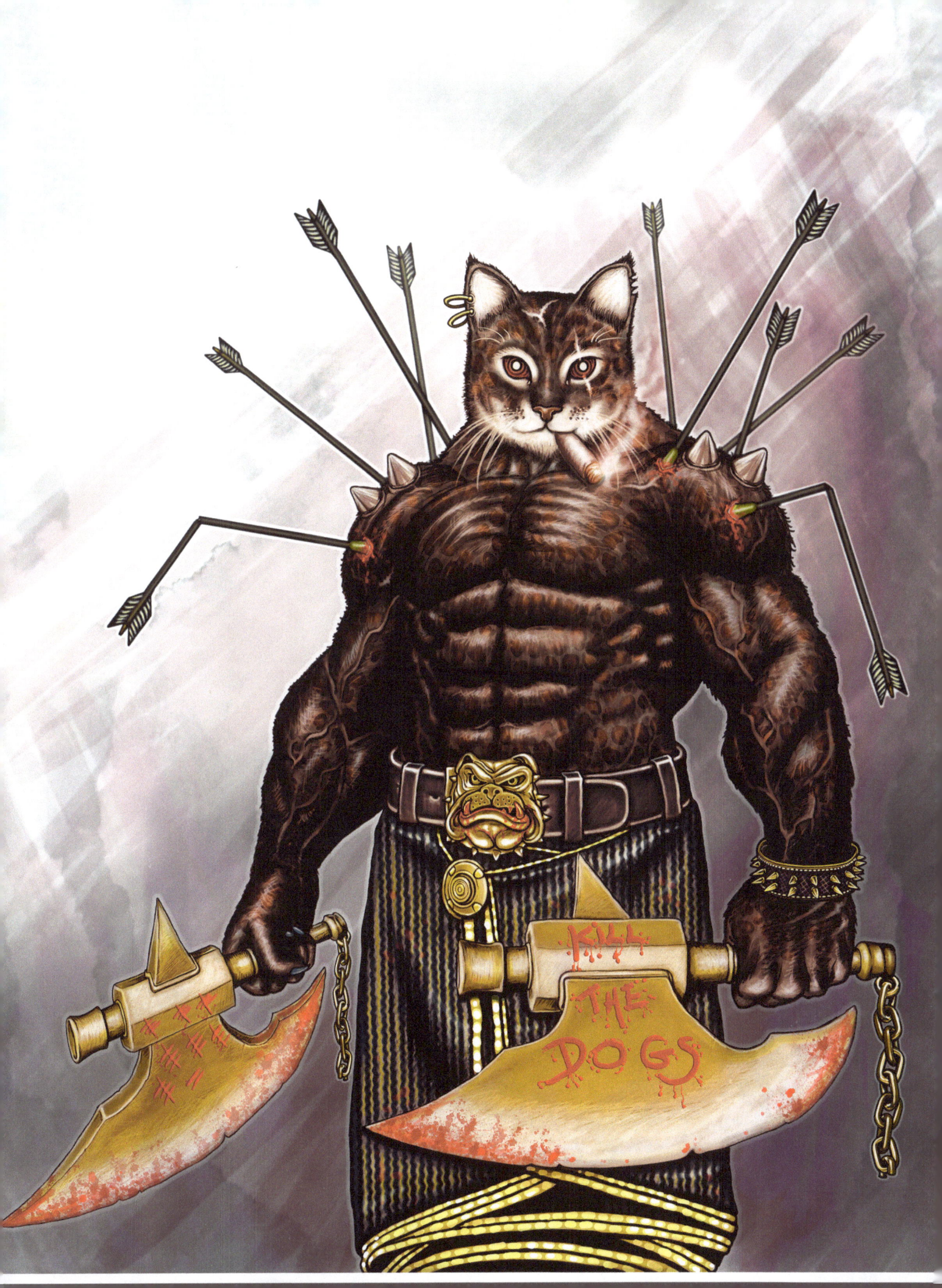

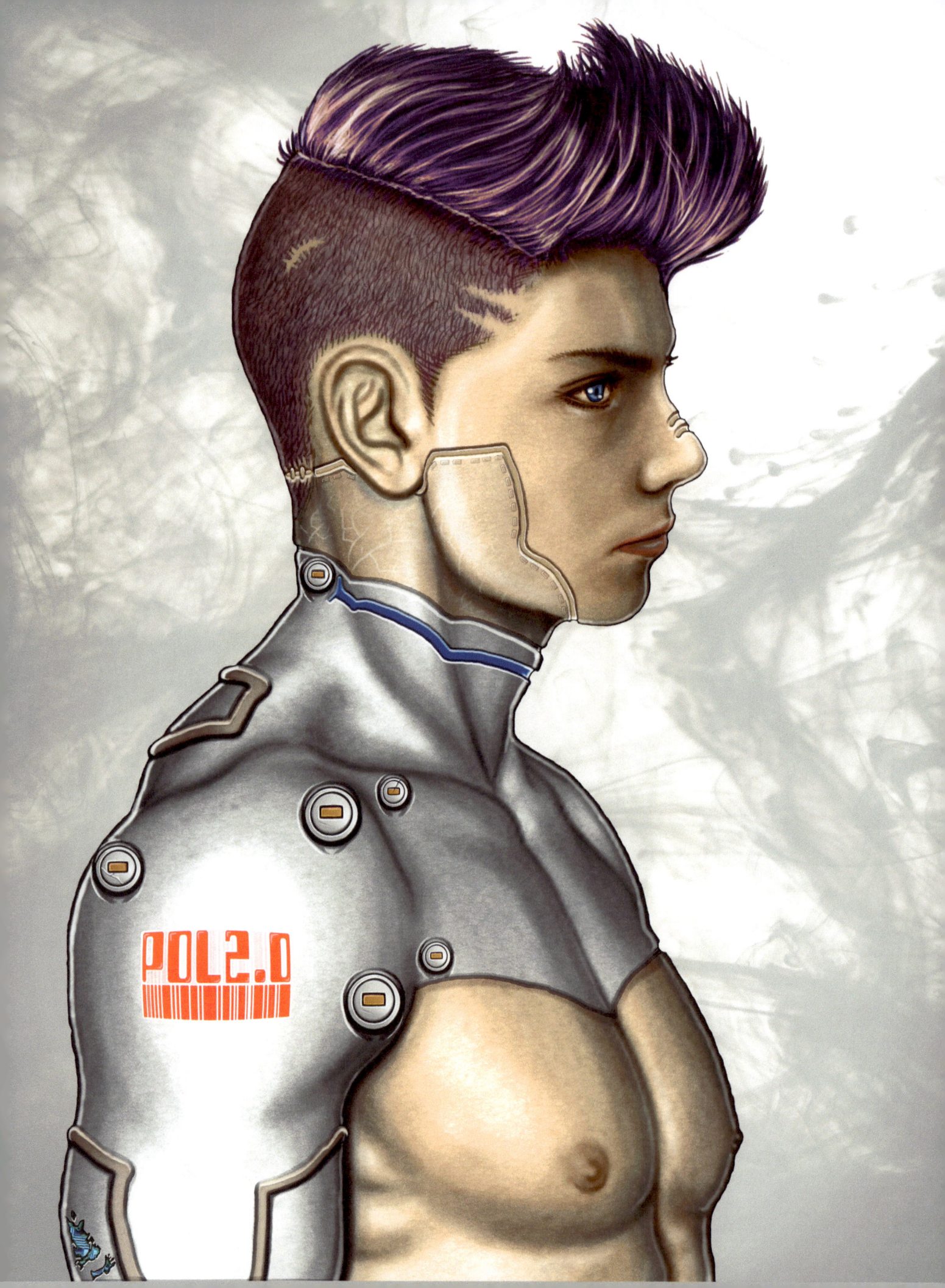

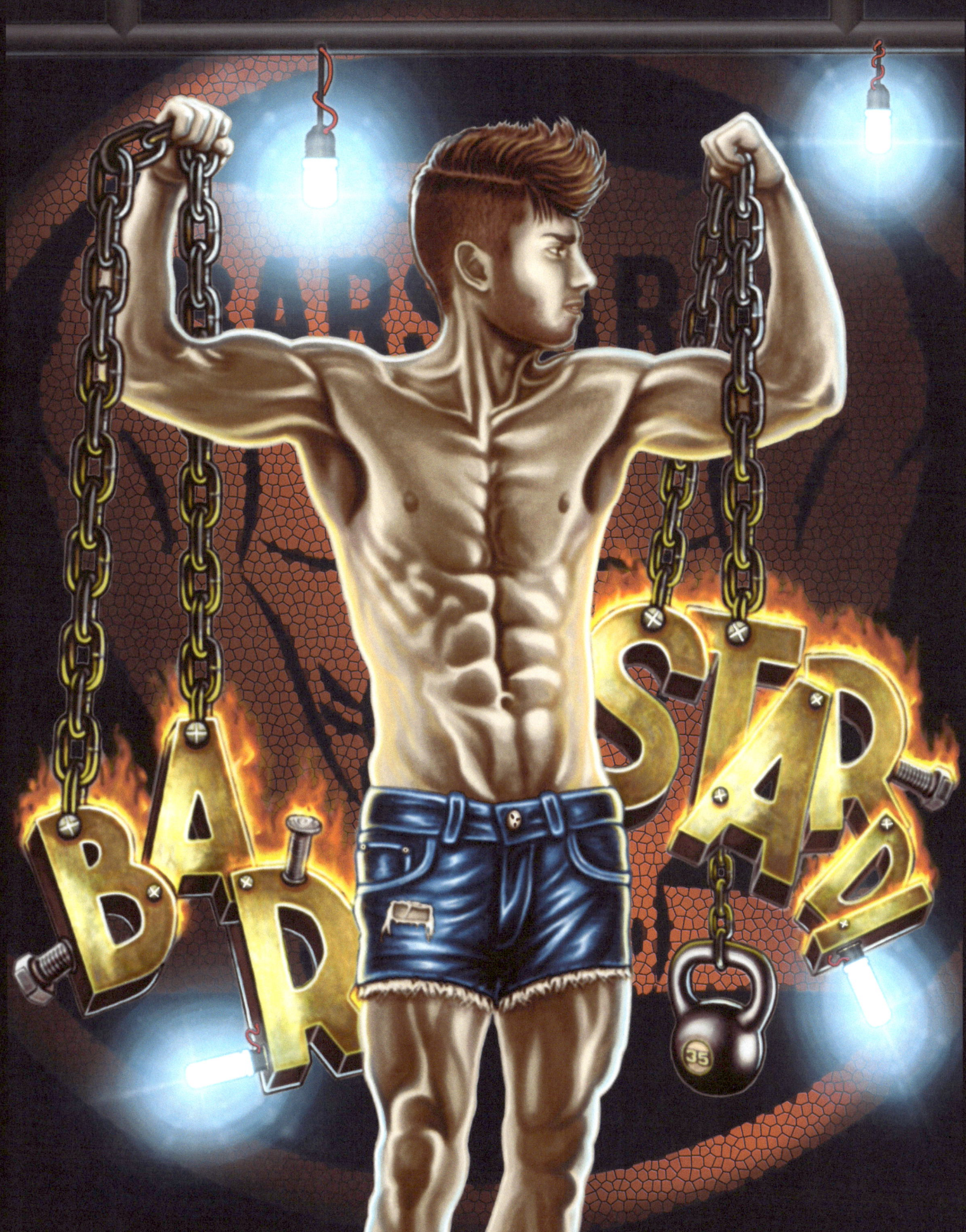

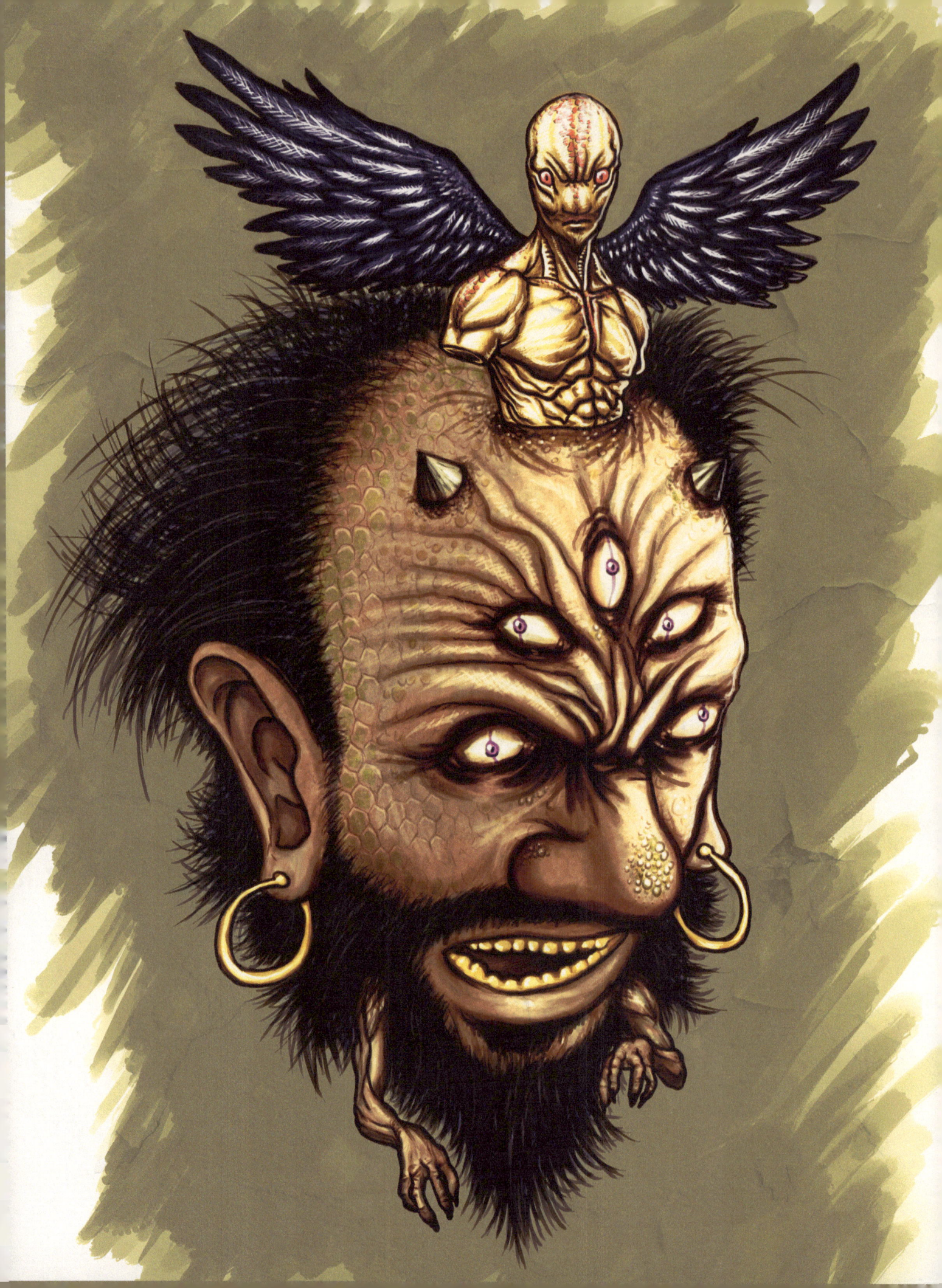

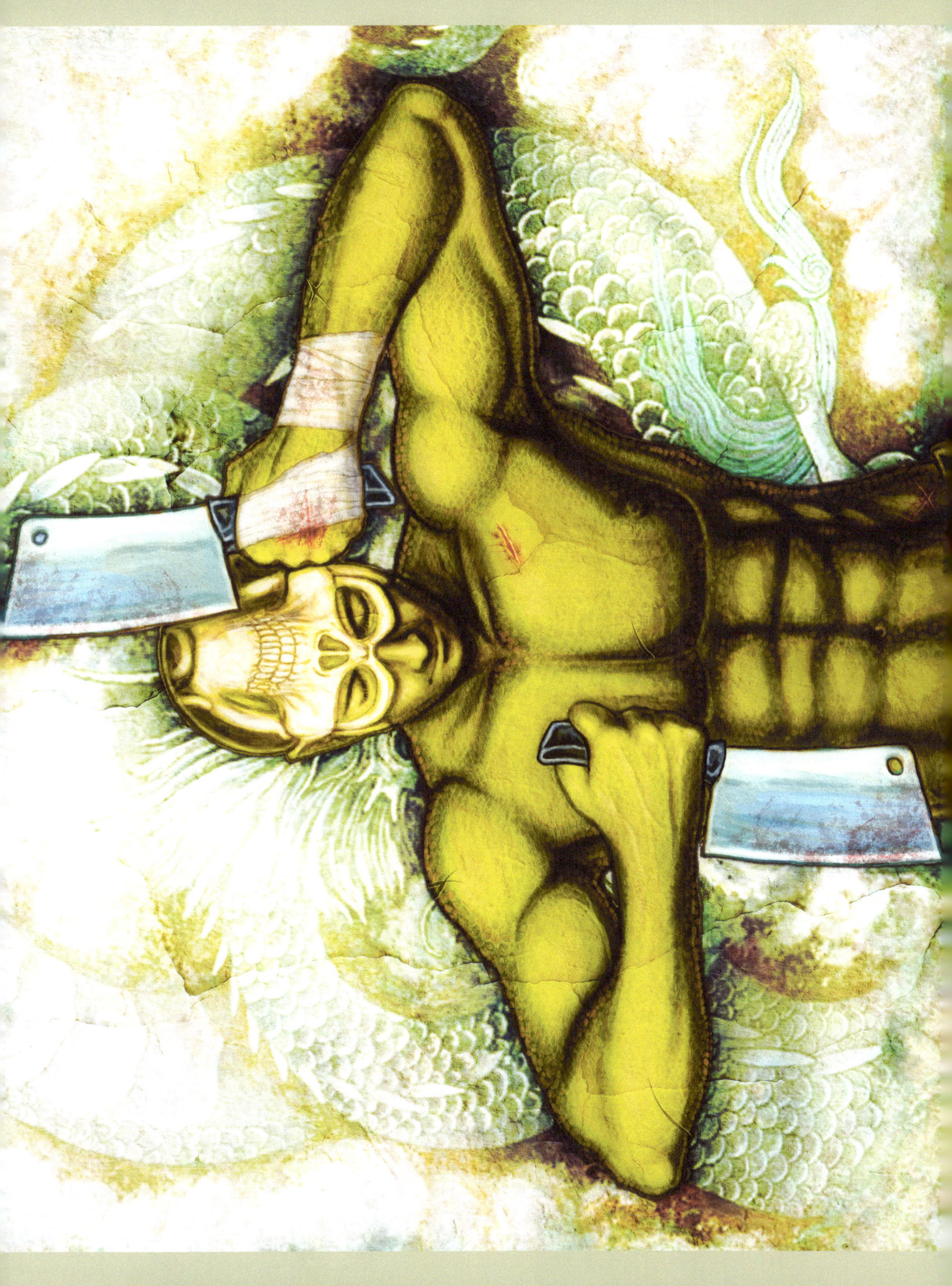

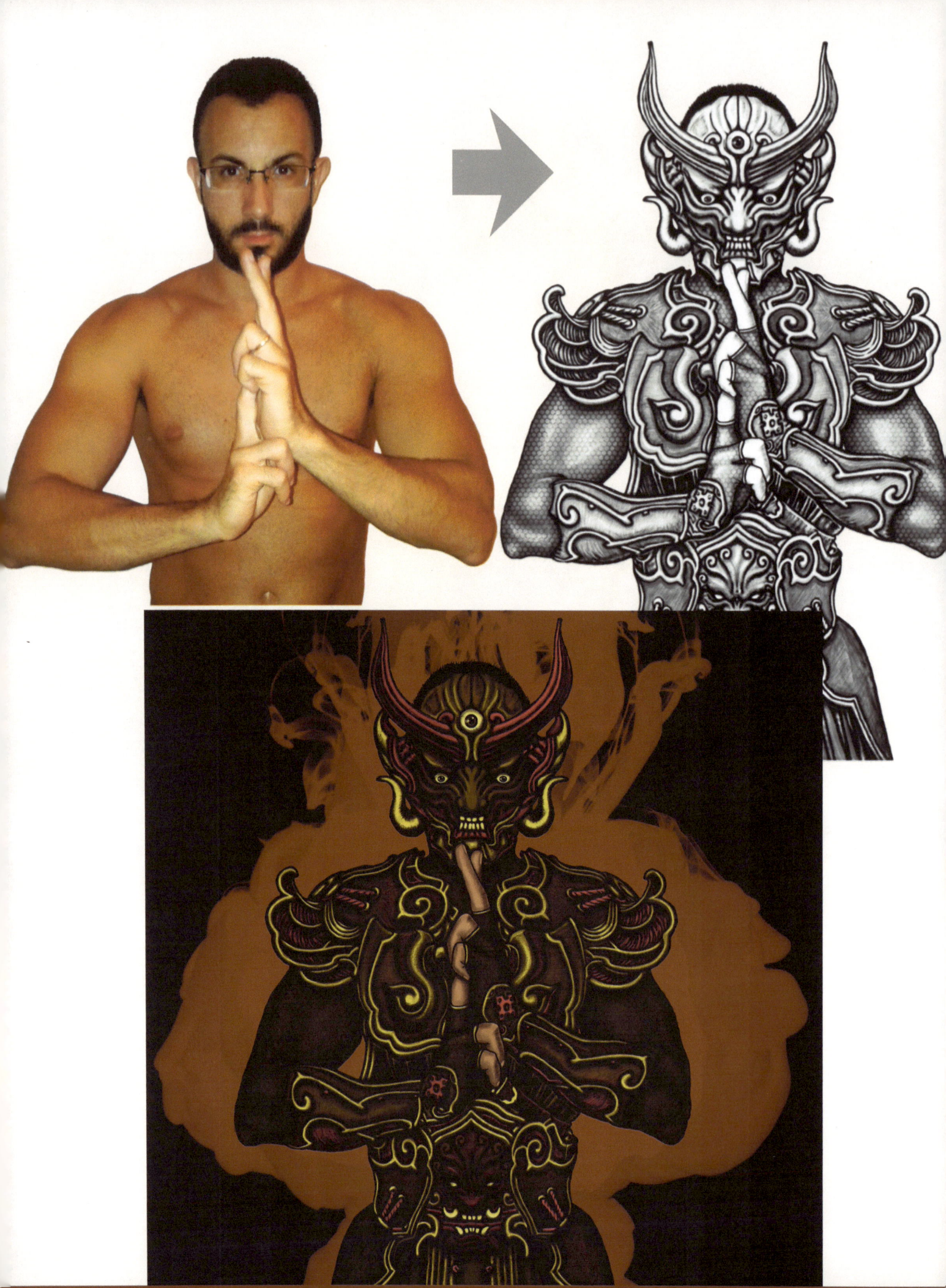

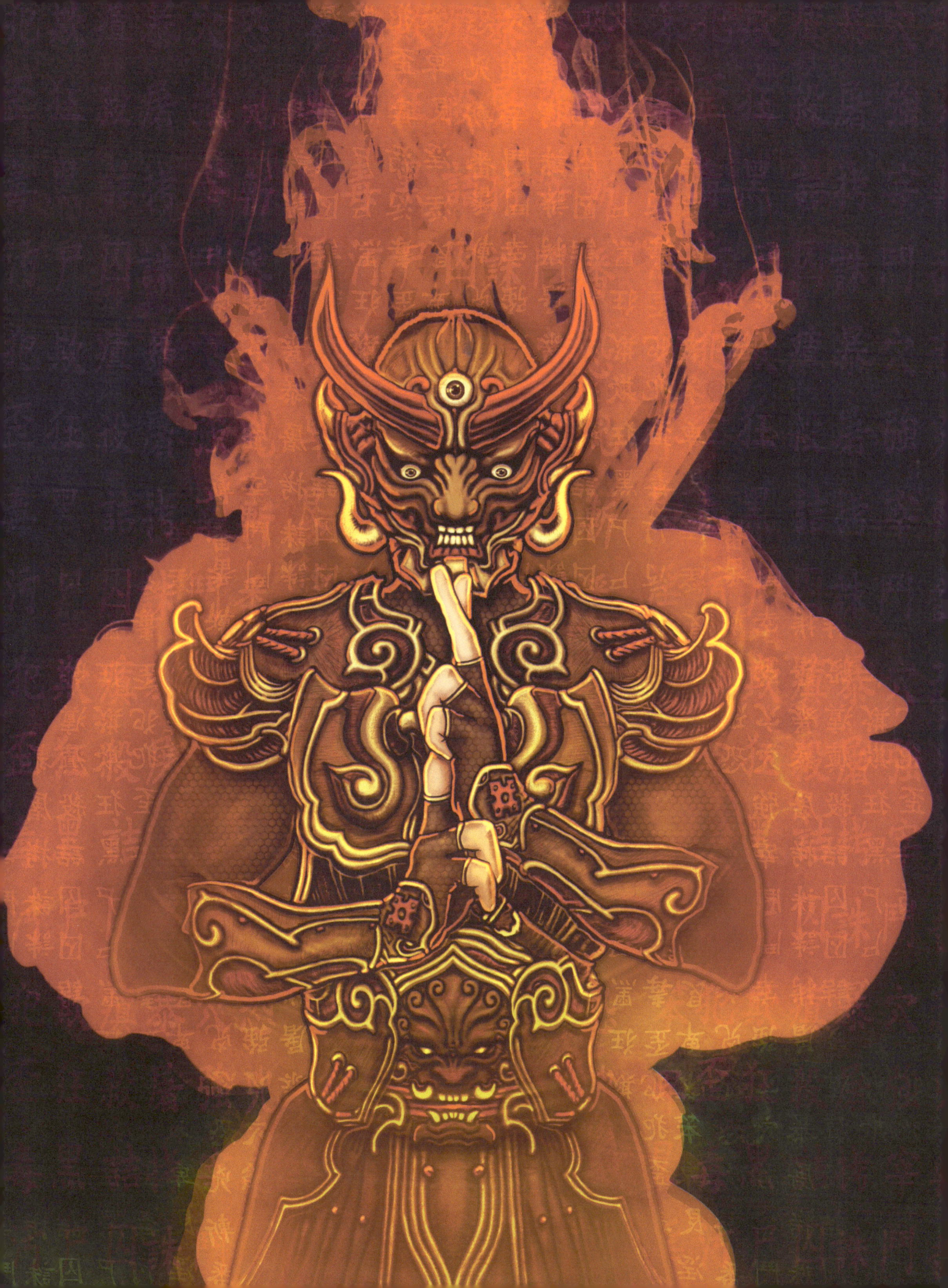

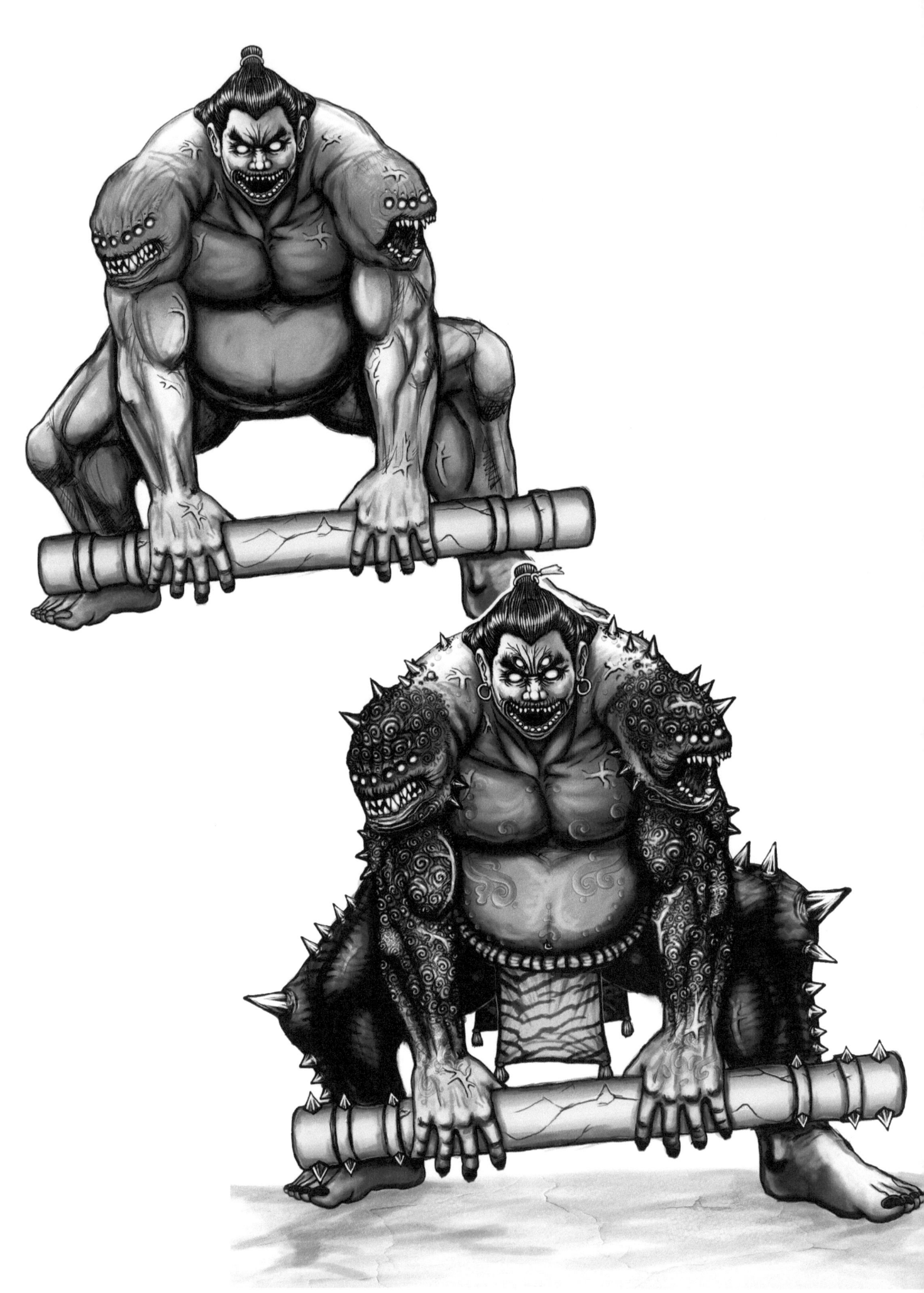

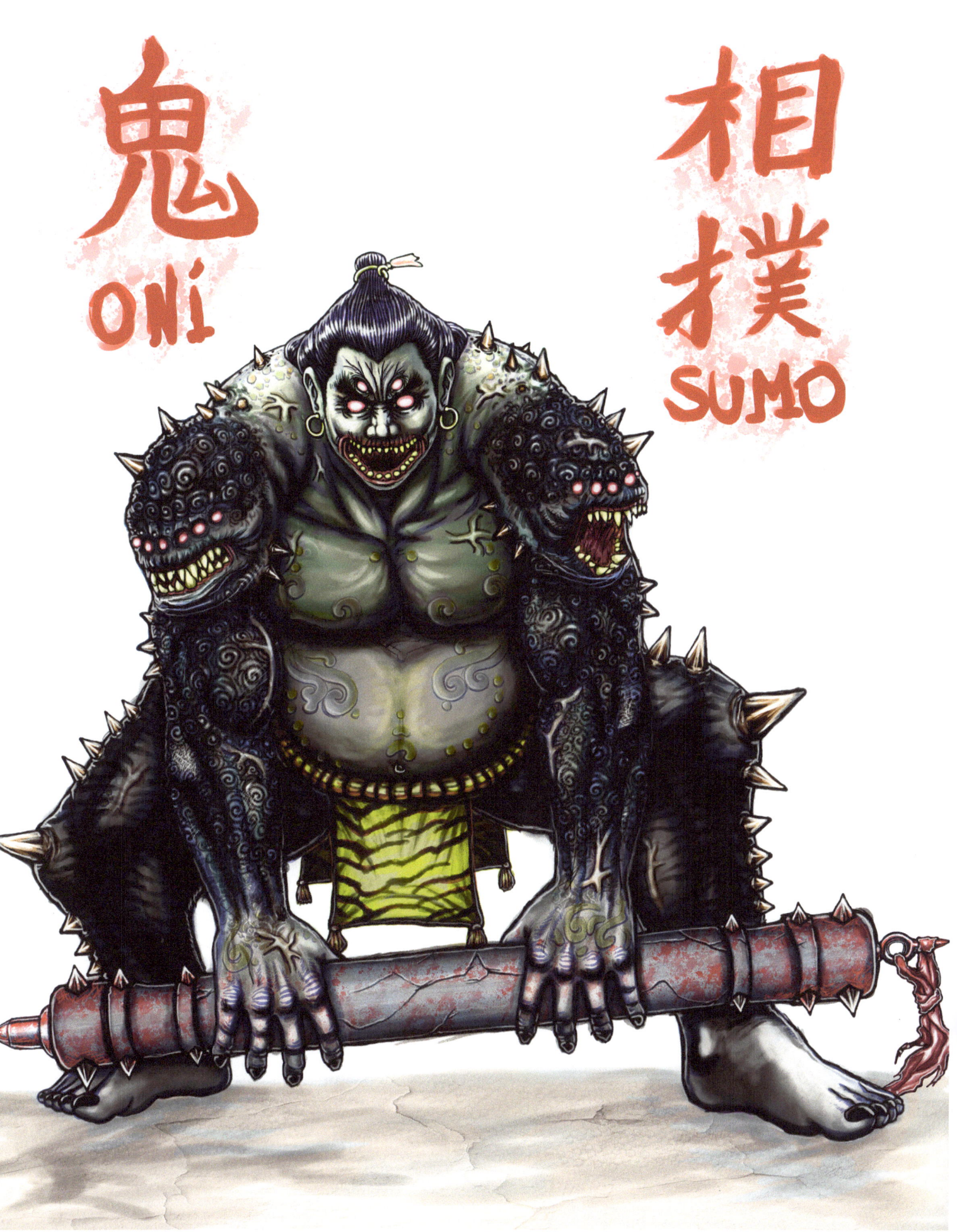
鬼
ONI

相撲
SUMO

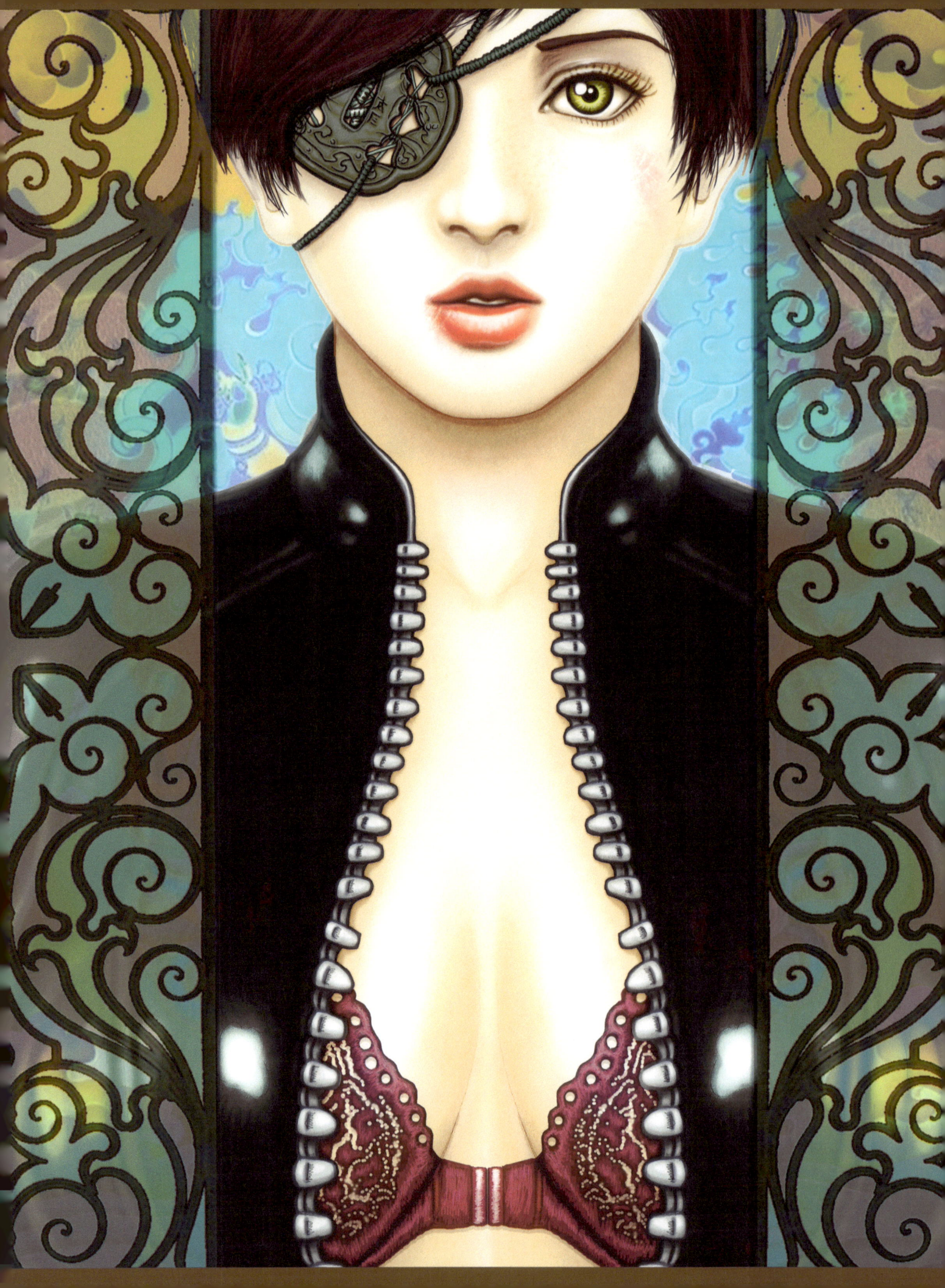

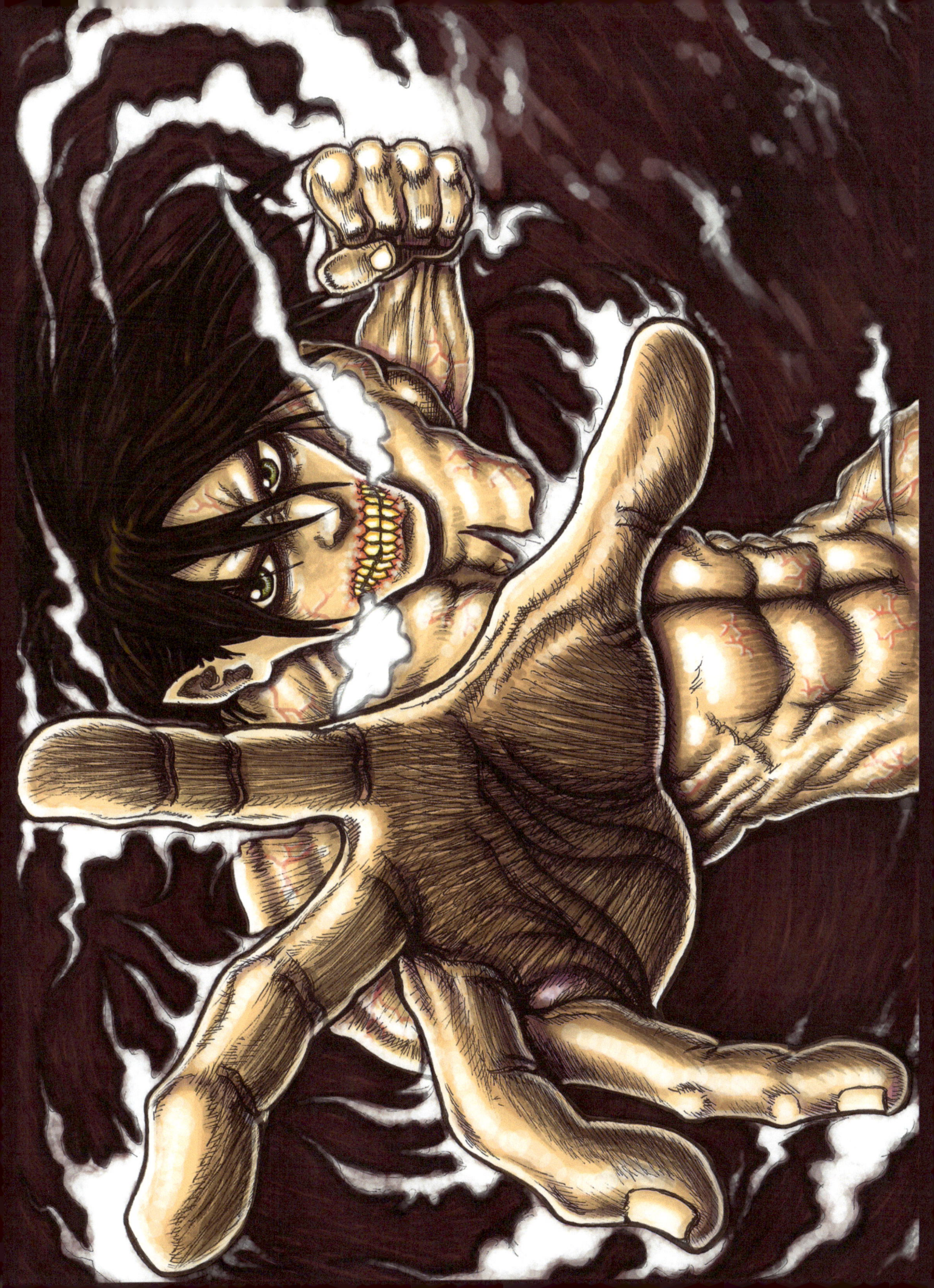

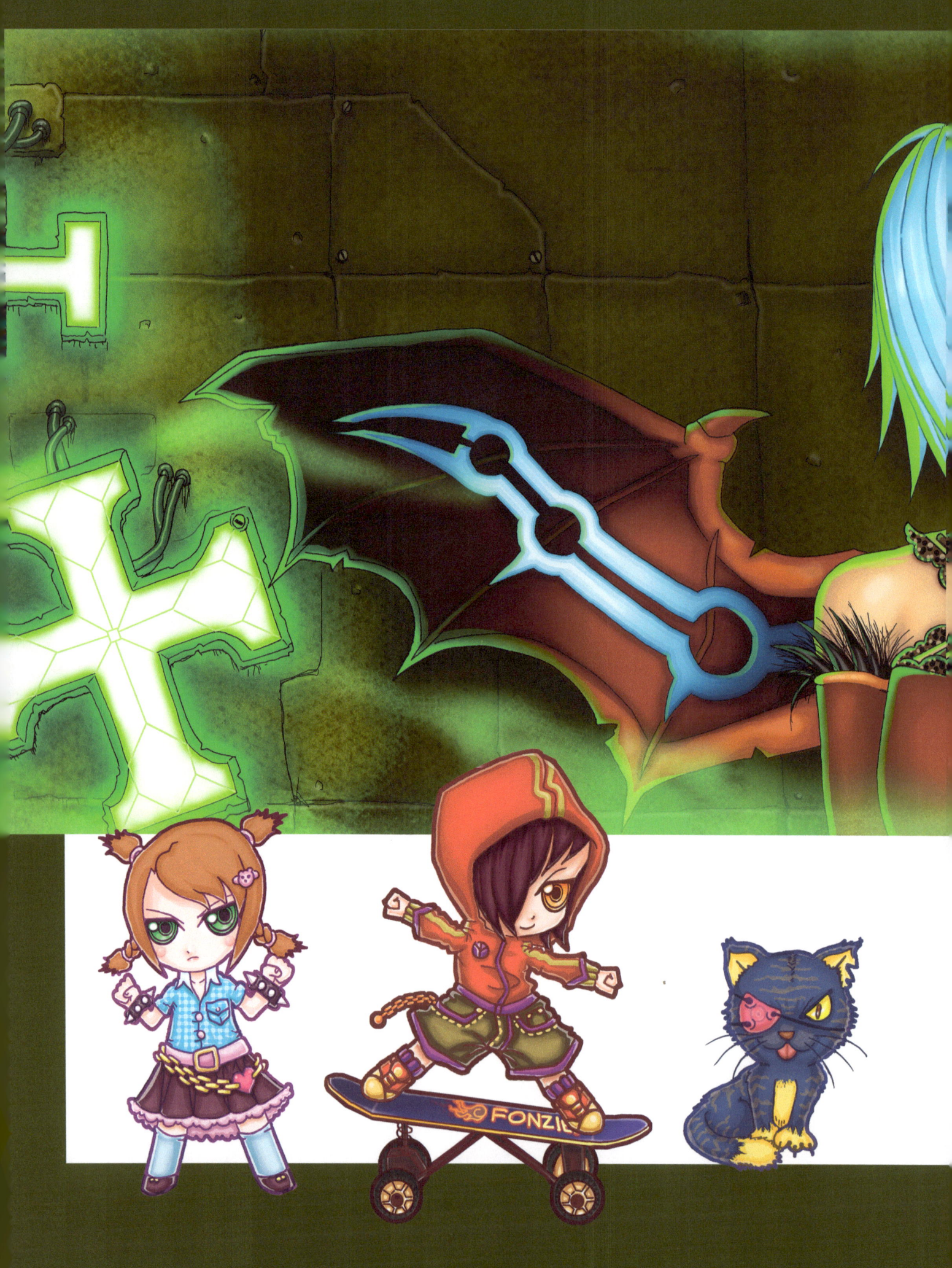

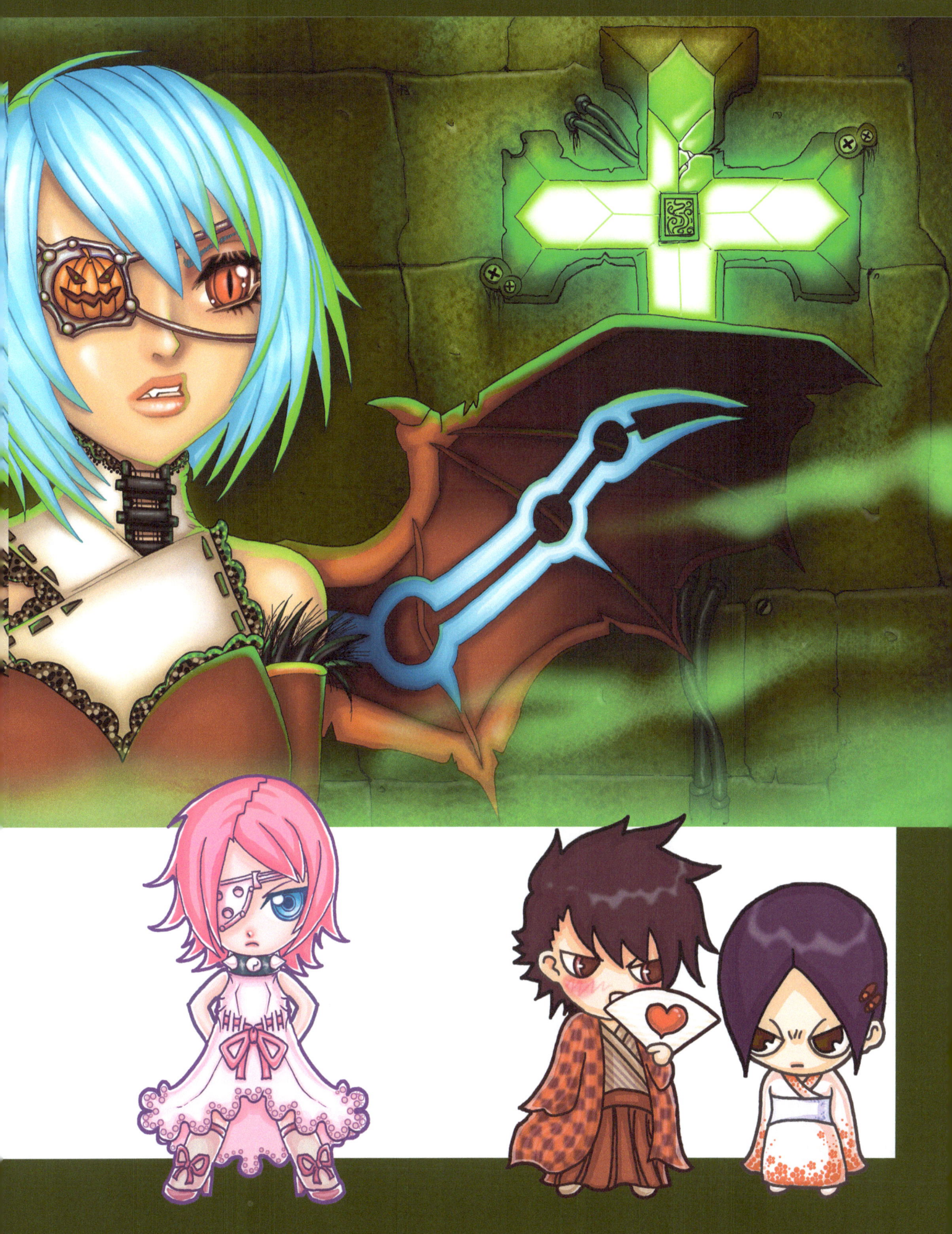

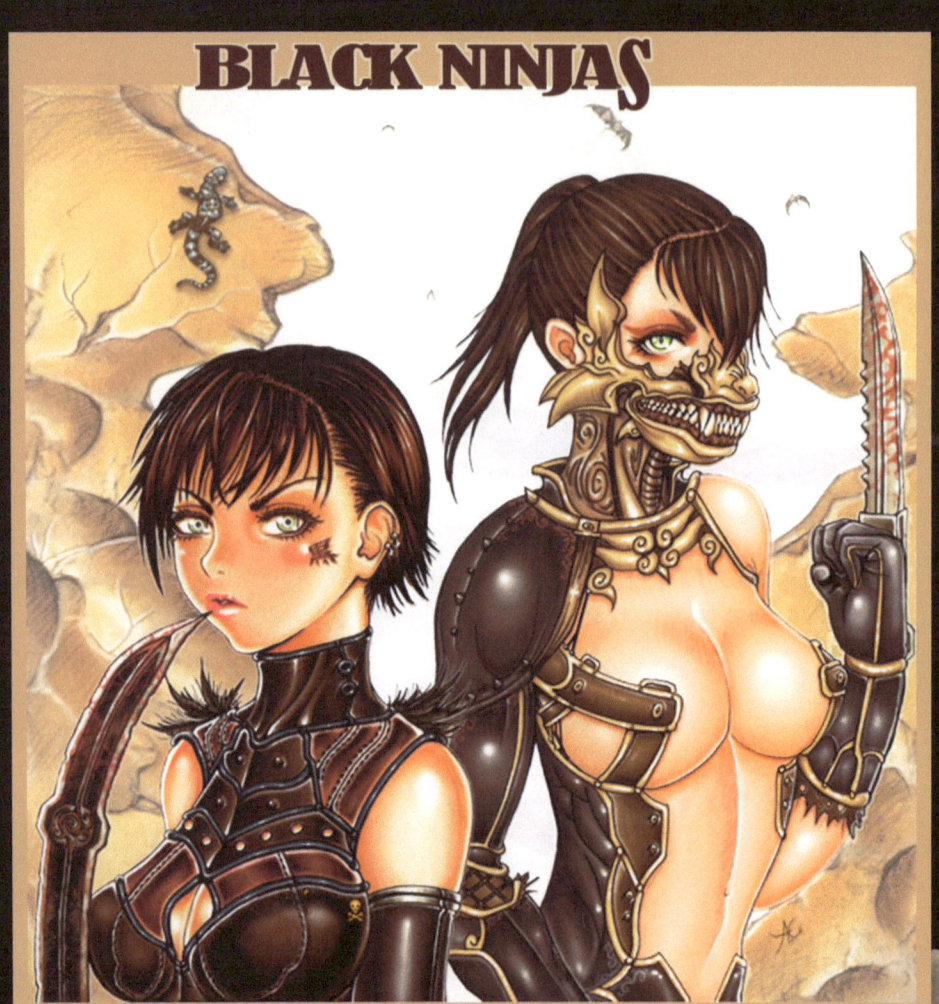

BLACK NINJAS

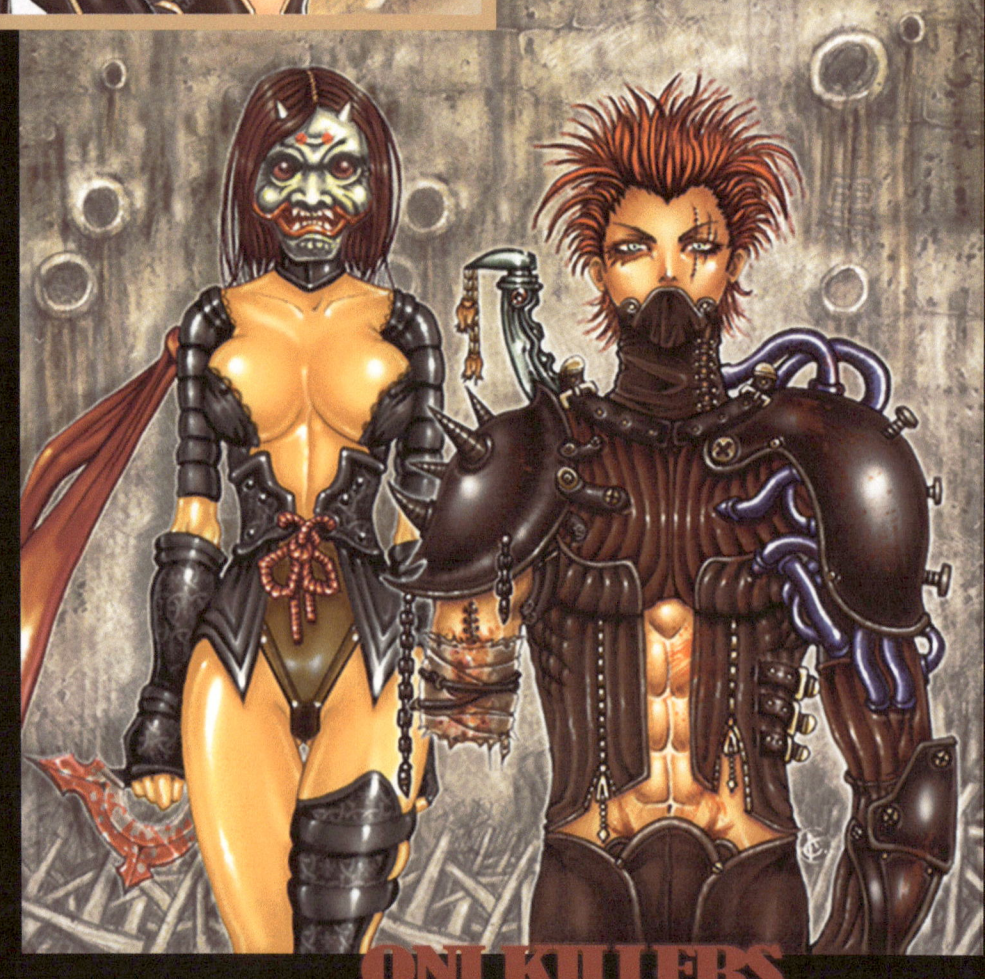

ONI KILLERS

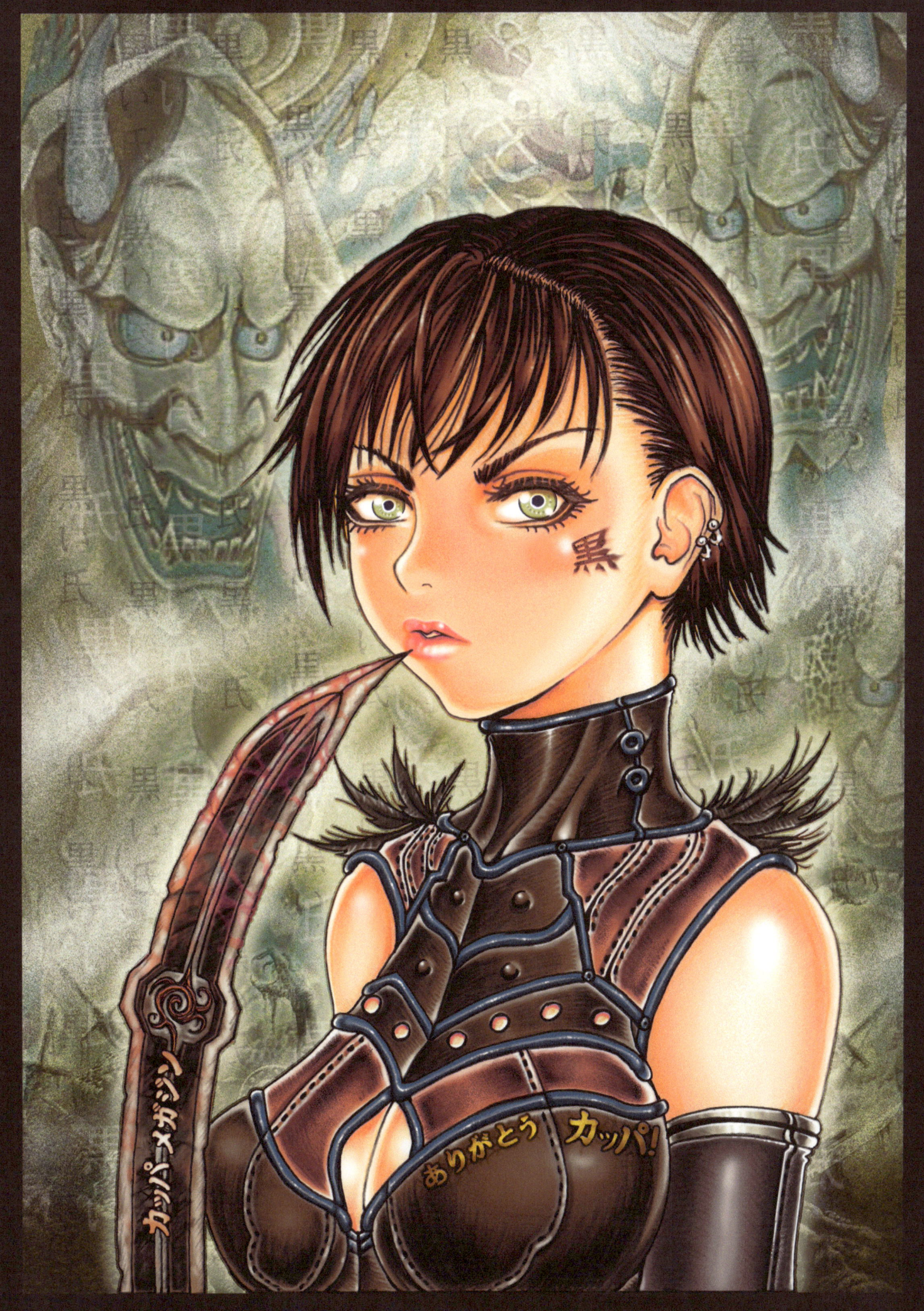

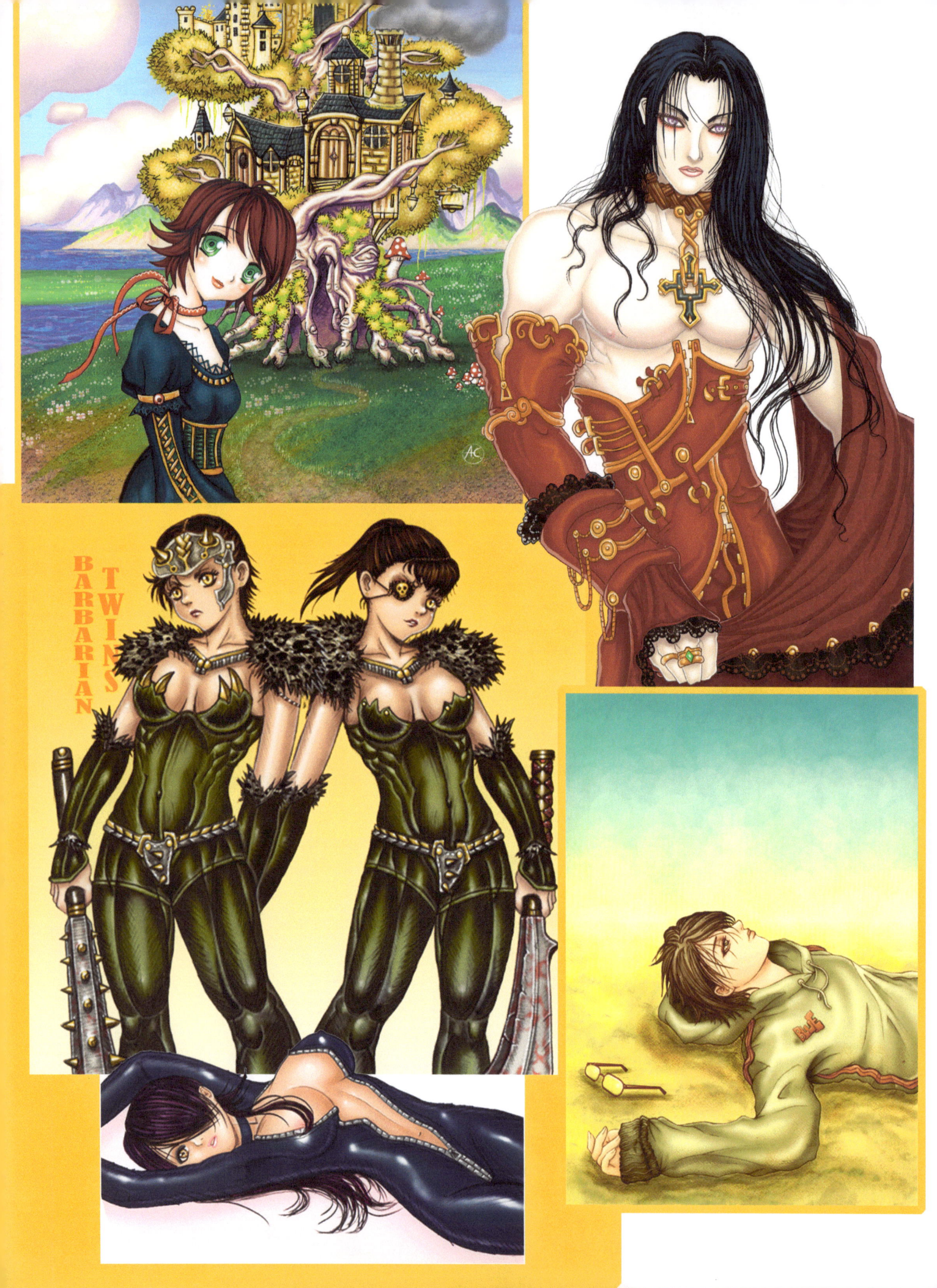

BARBARIAN TWINS

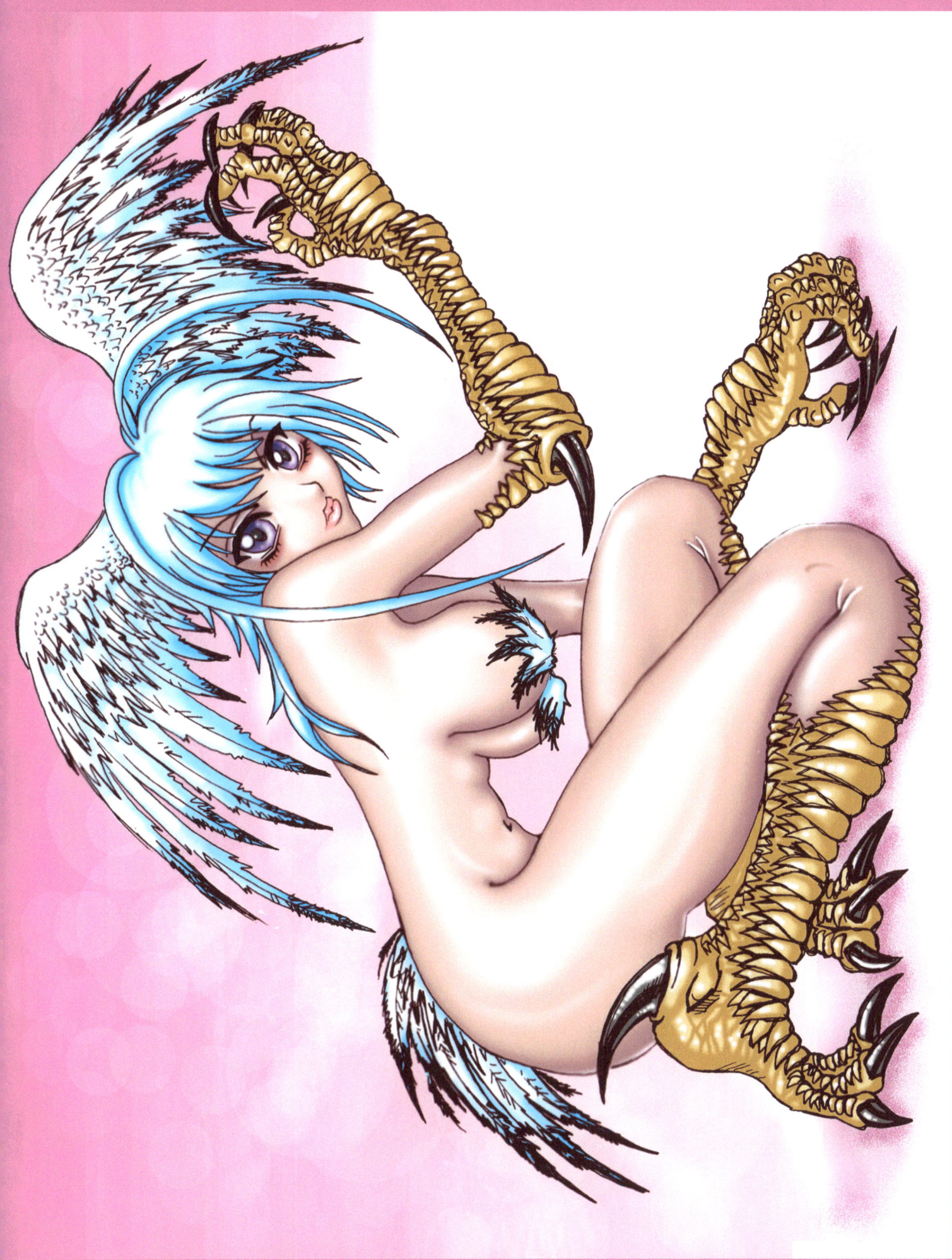

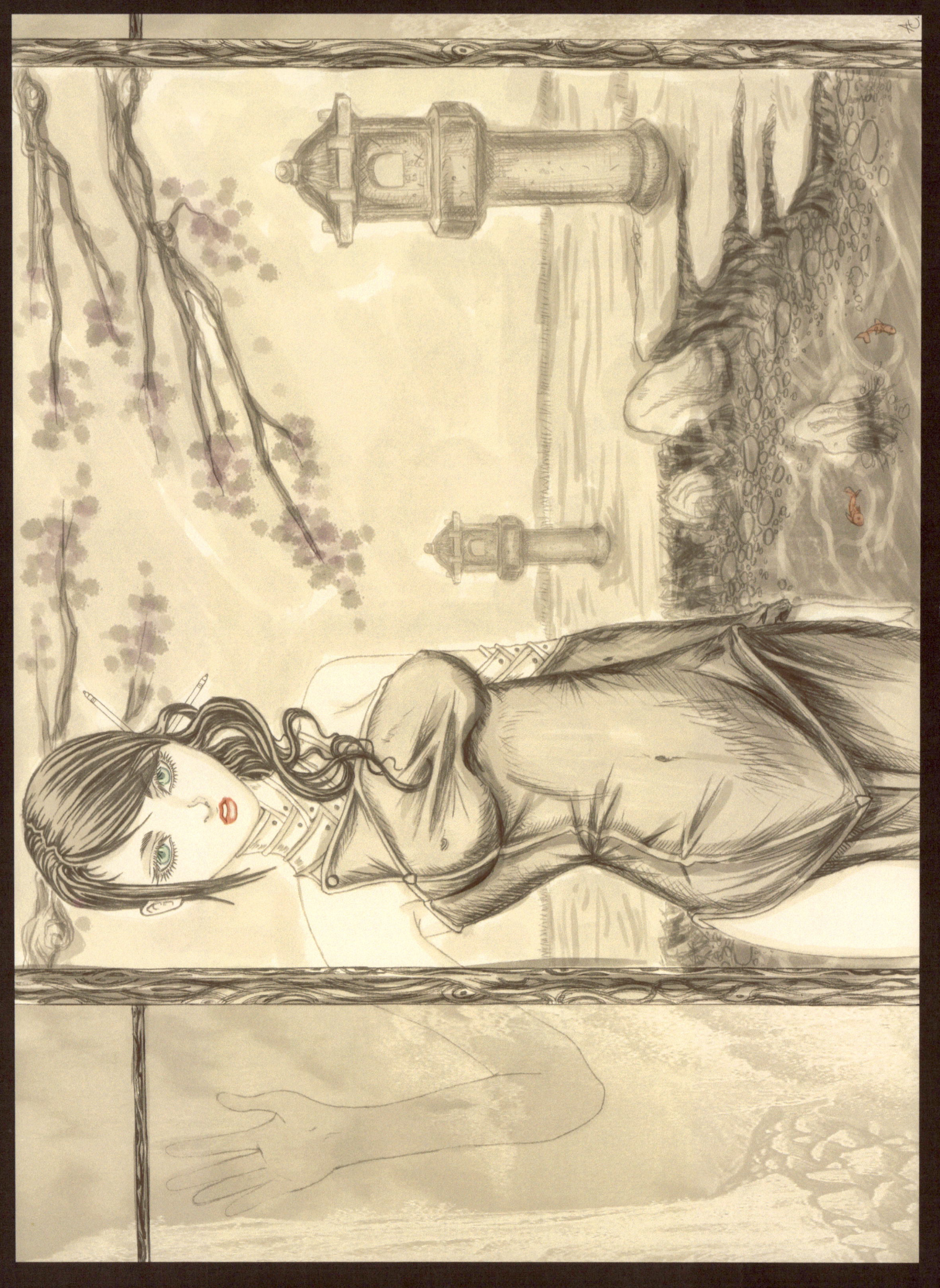

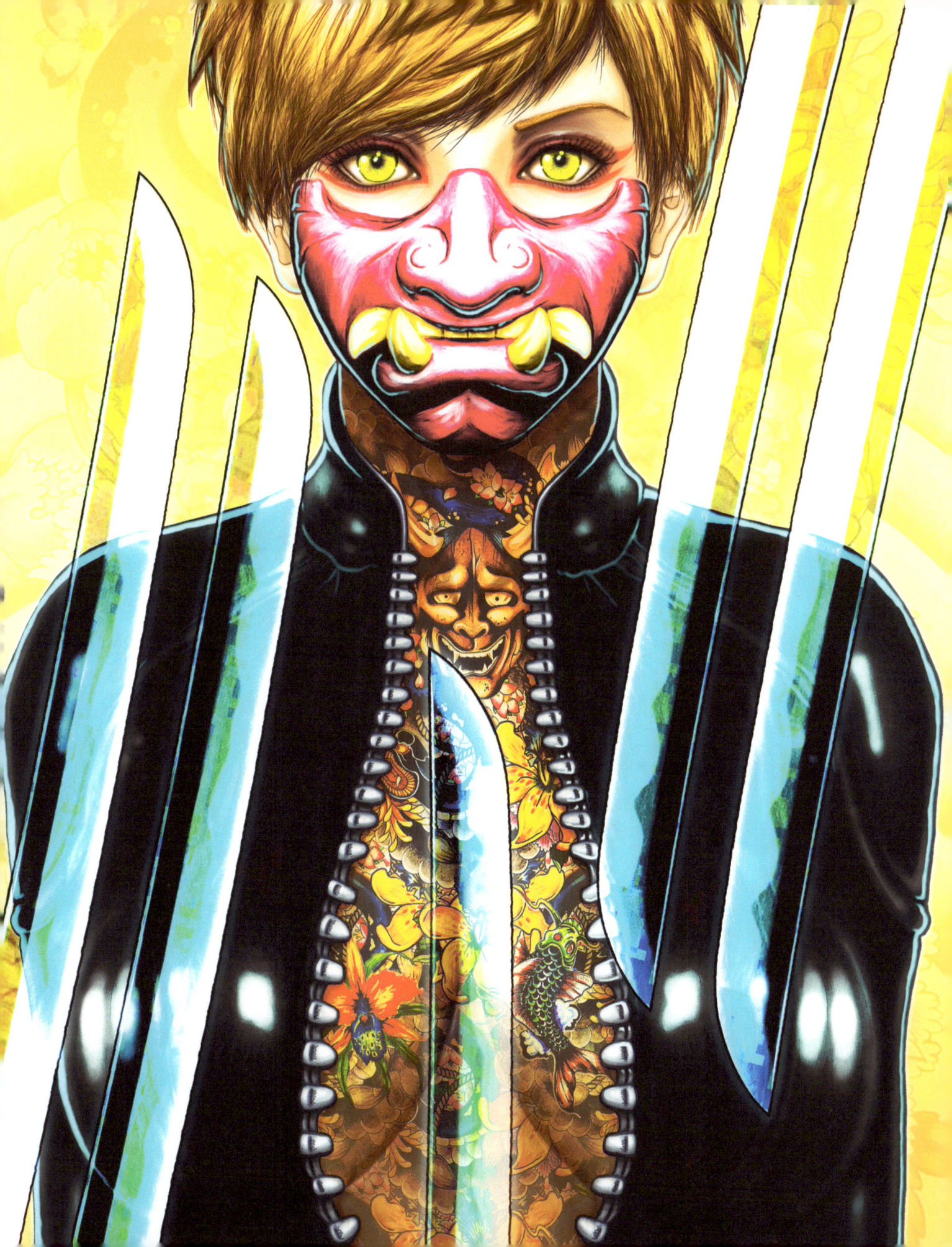

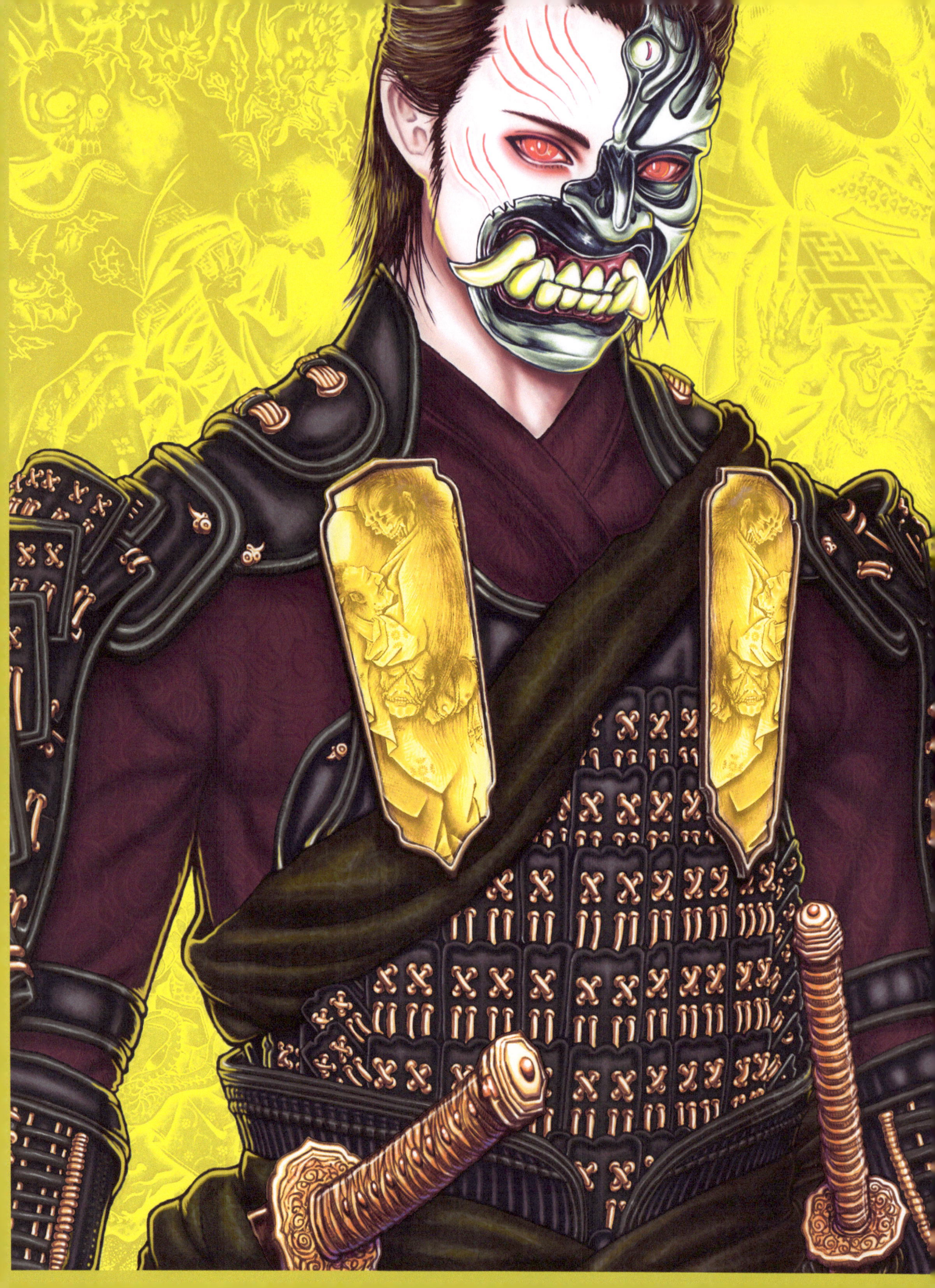

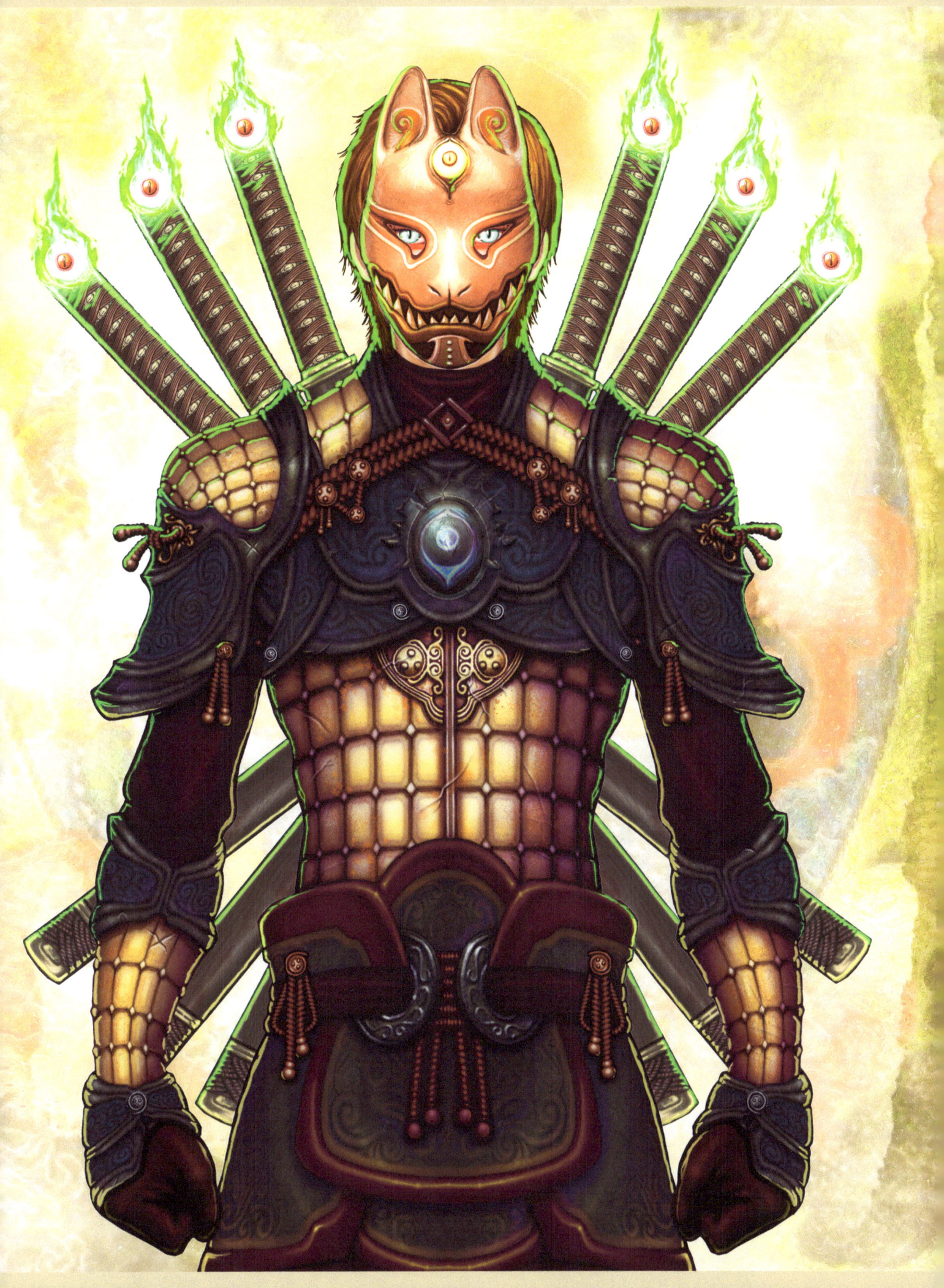

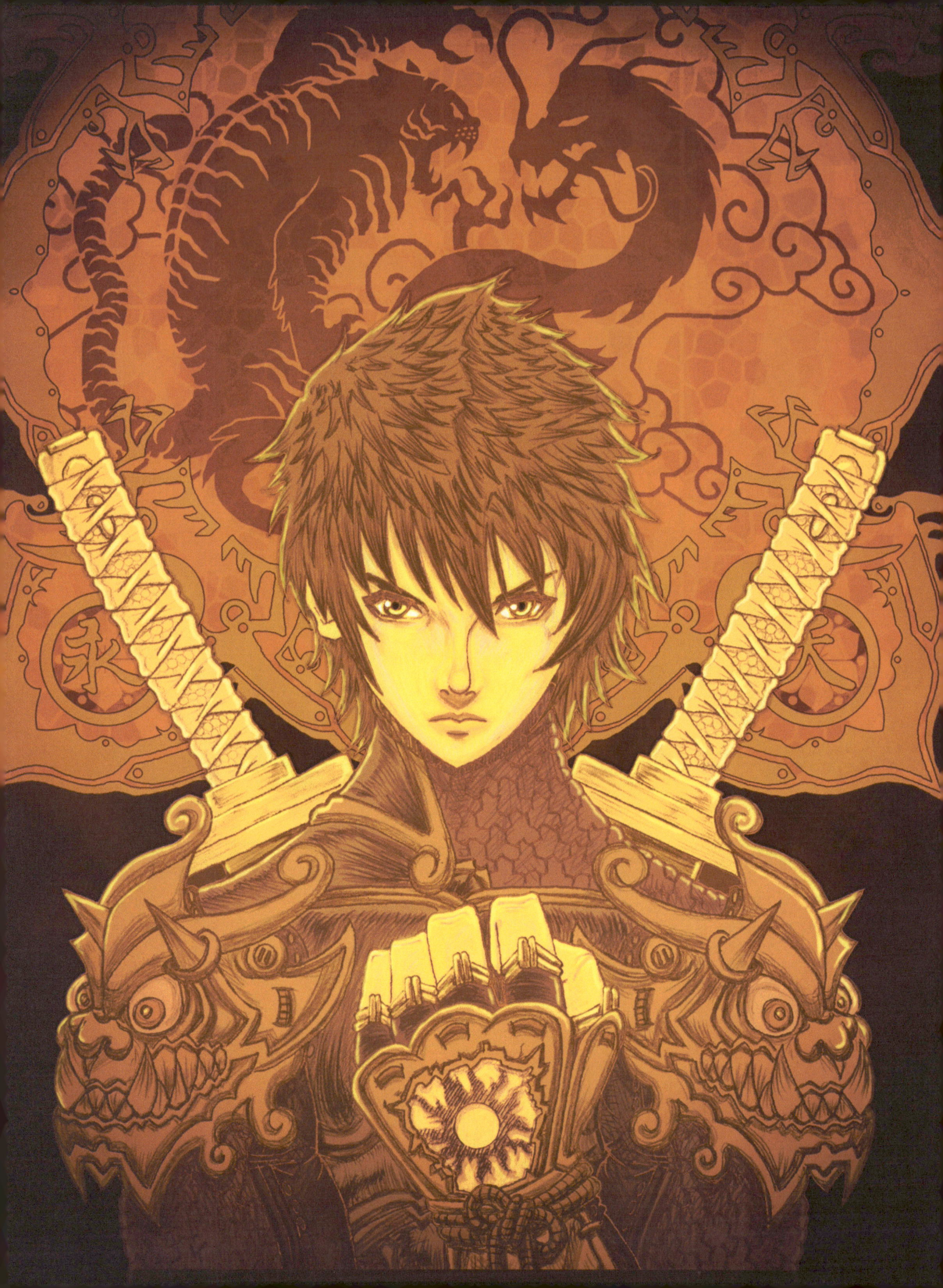

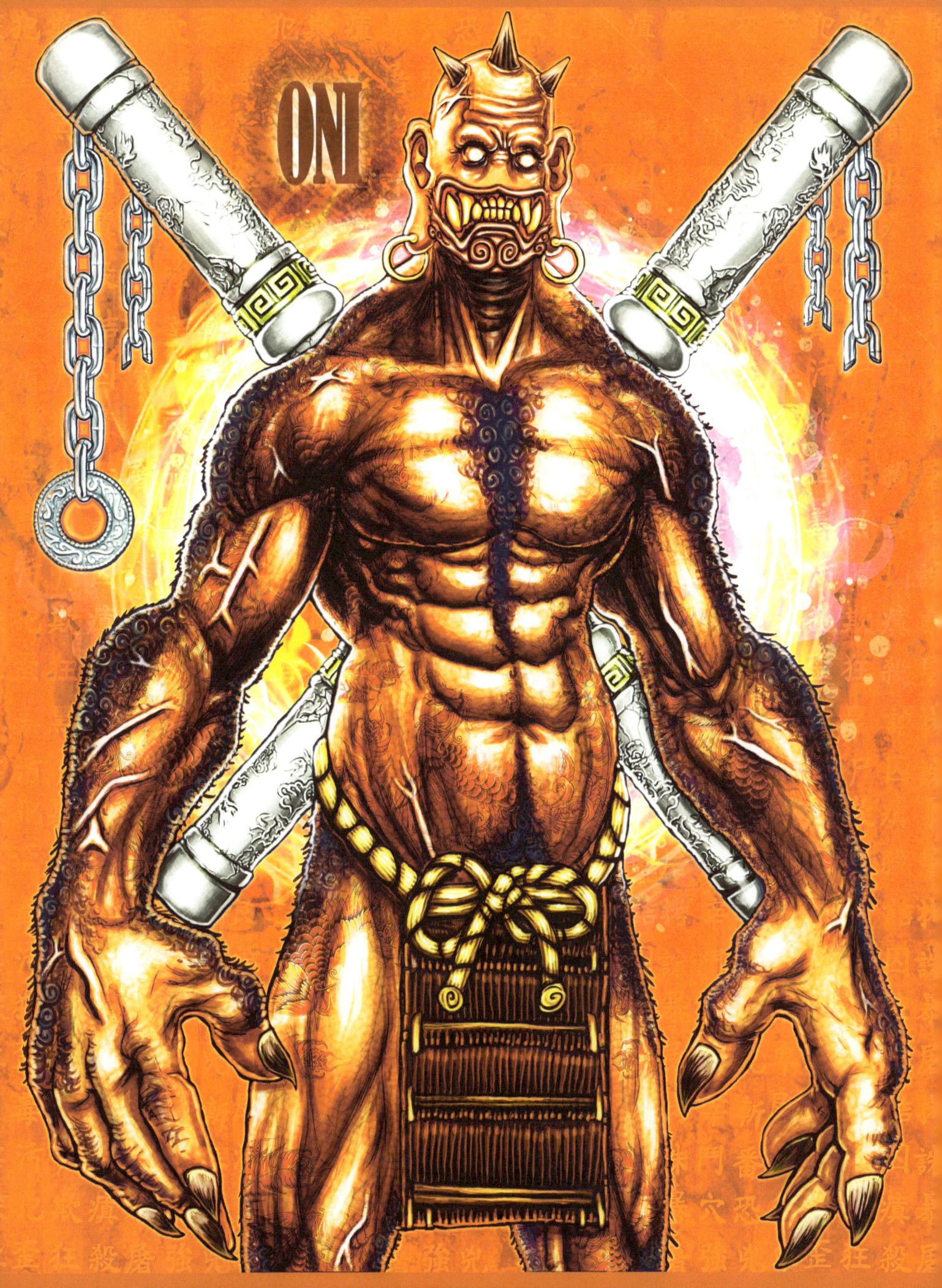

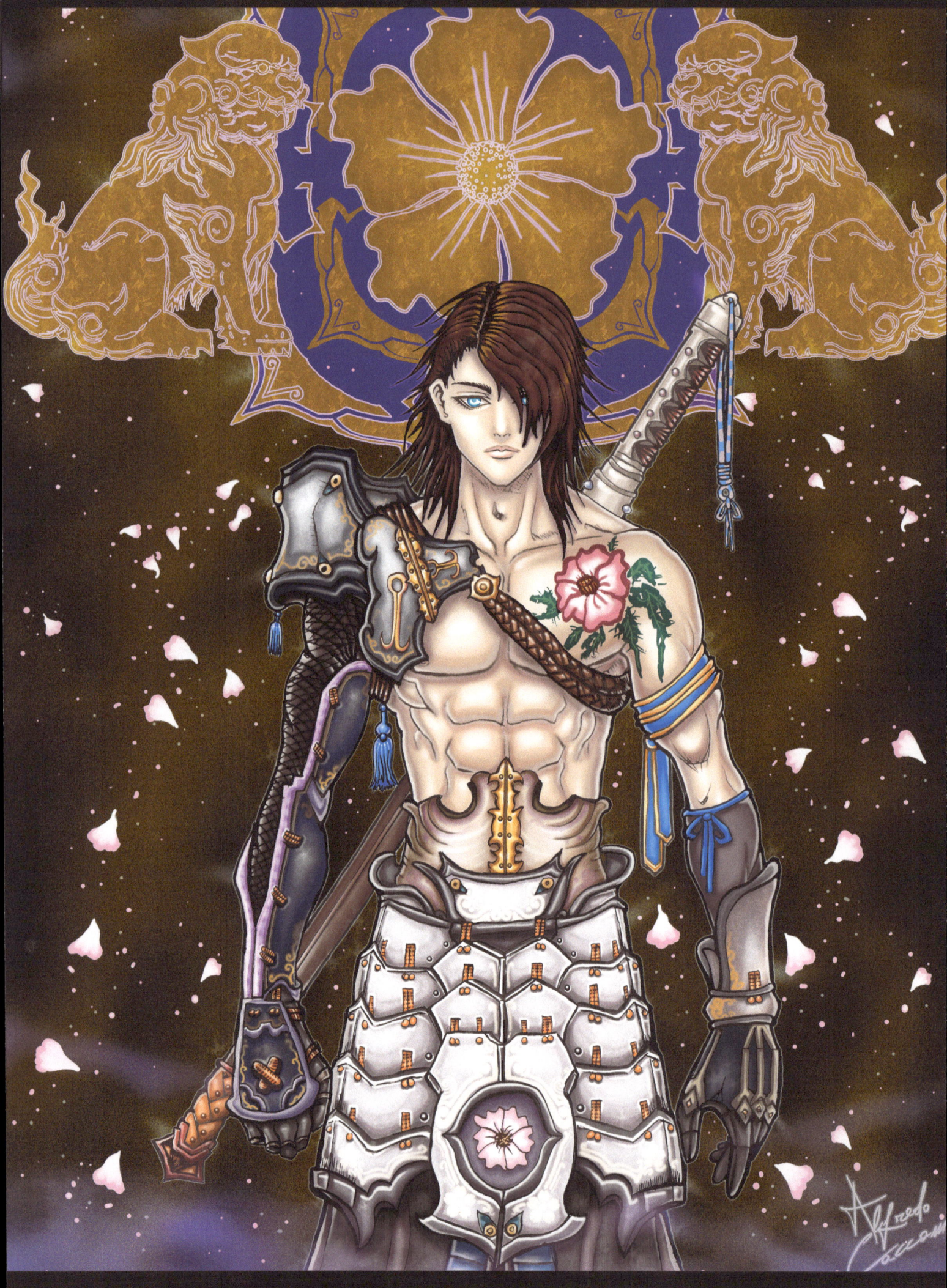

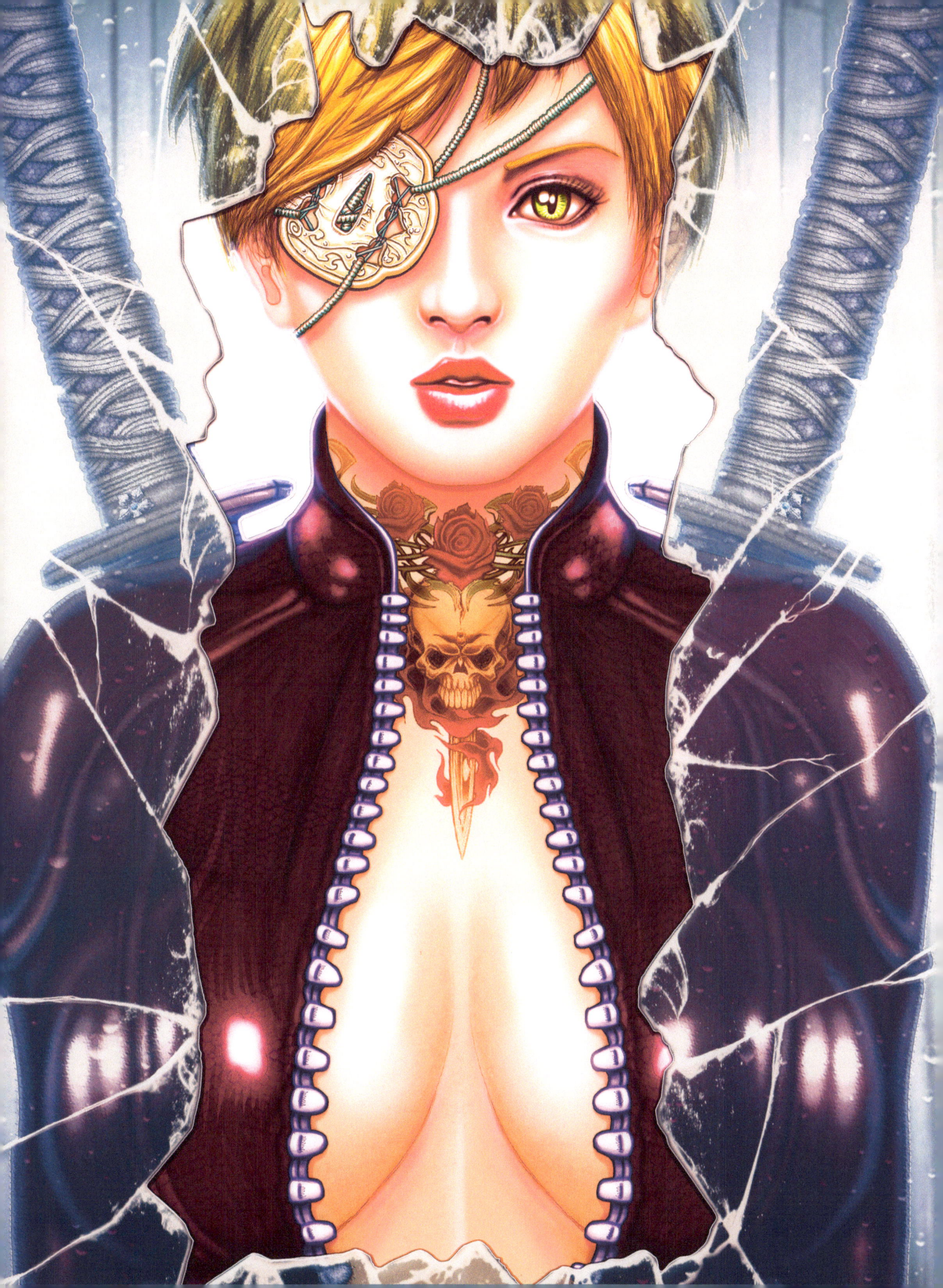

REFERENCES

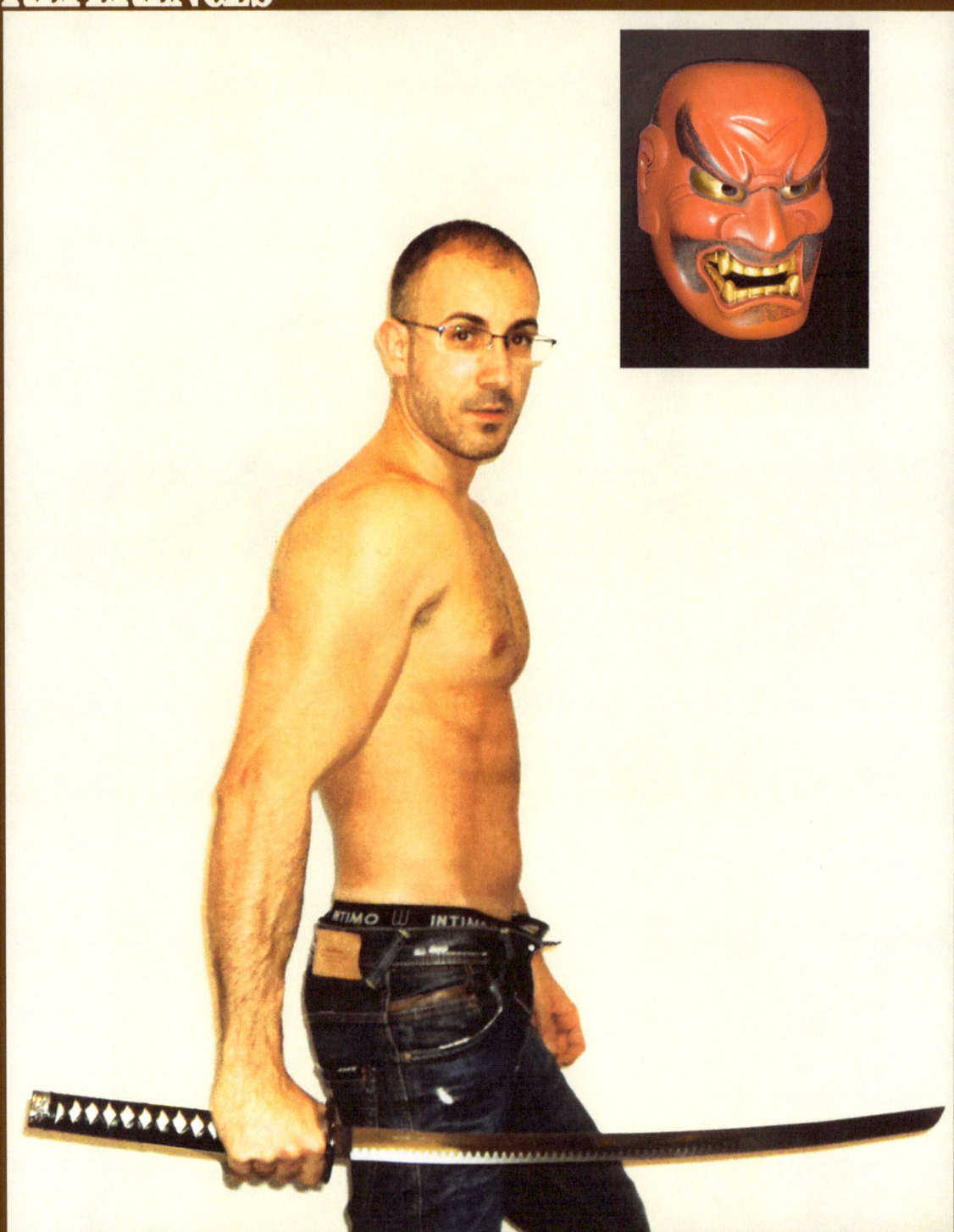

ME & MASK (PHOTOS)

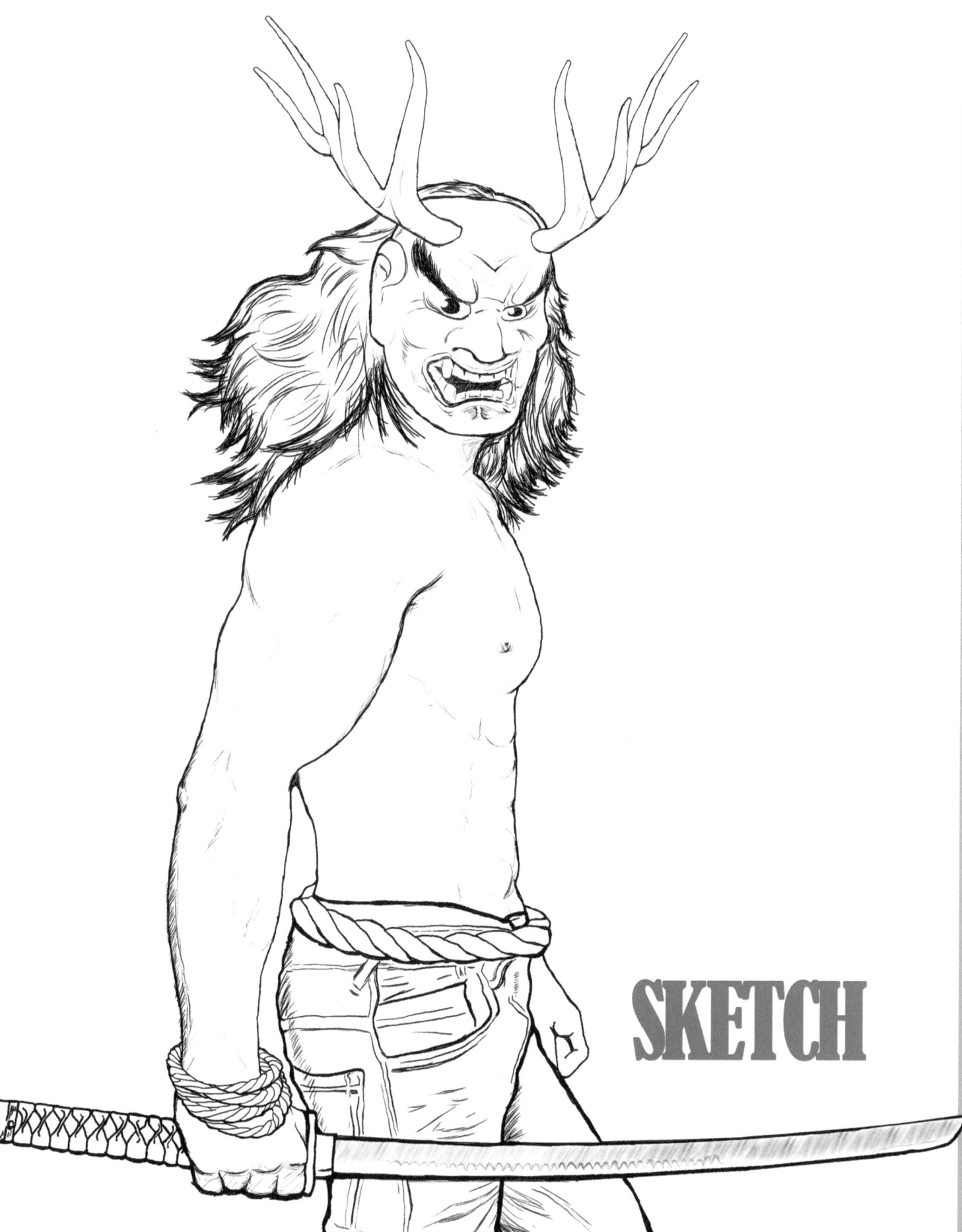

SKETCH

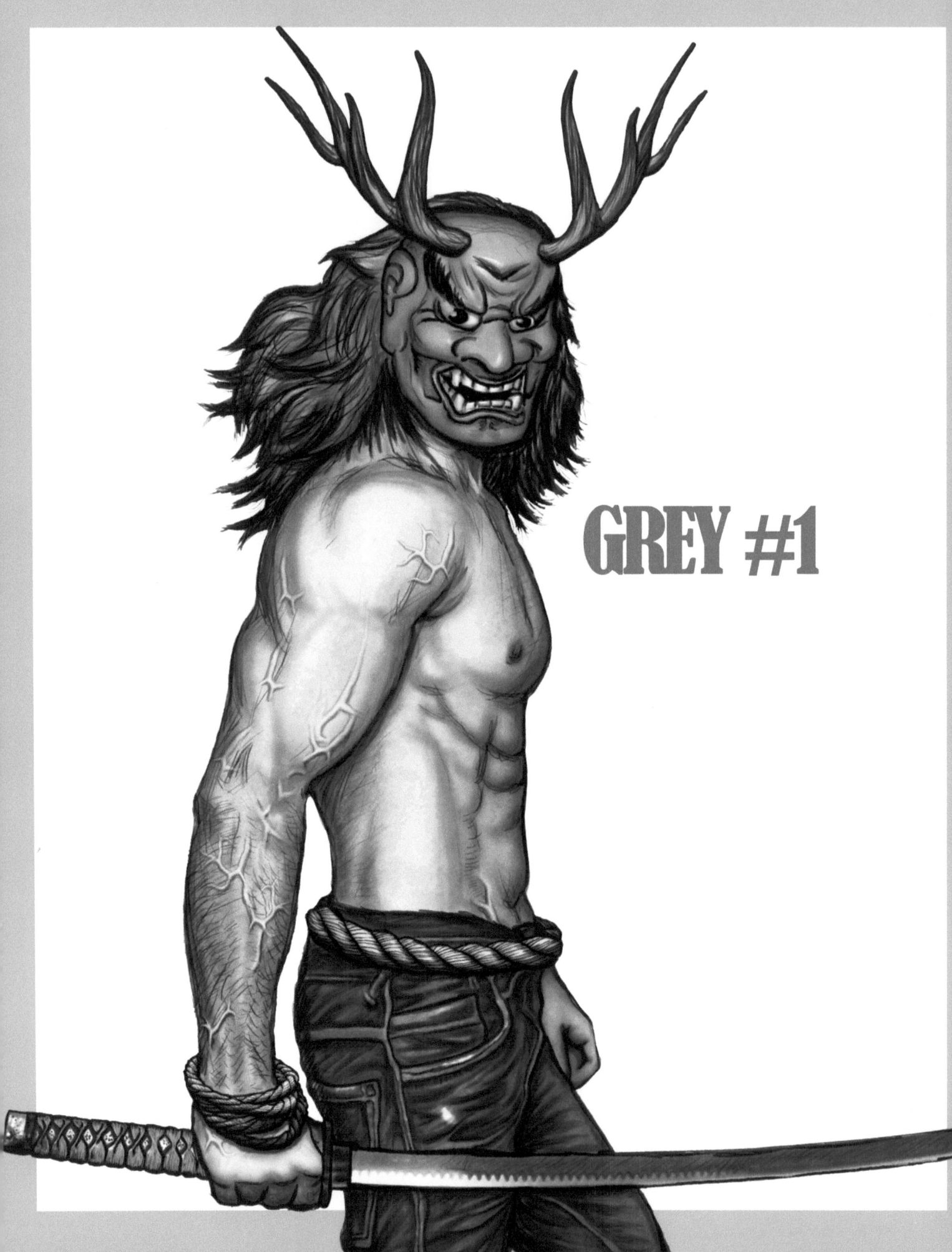

GREY #1

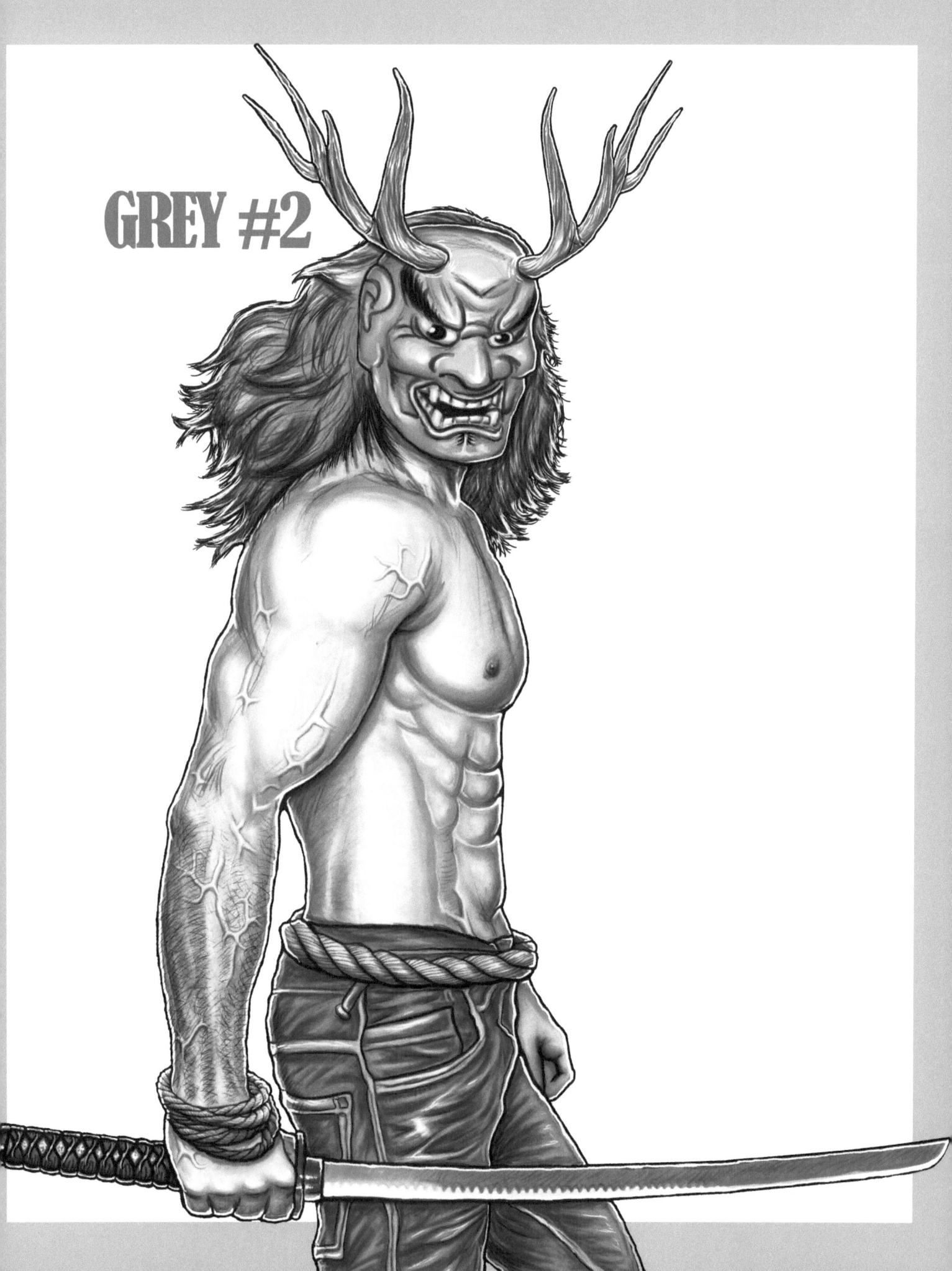

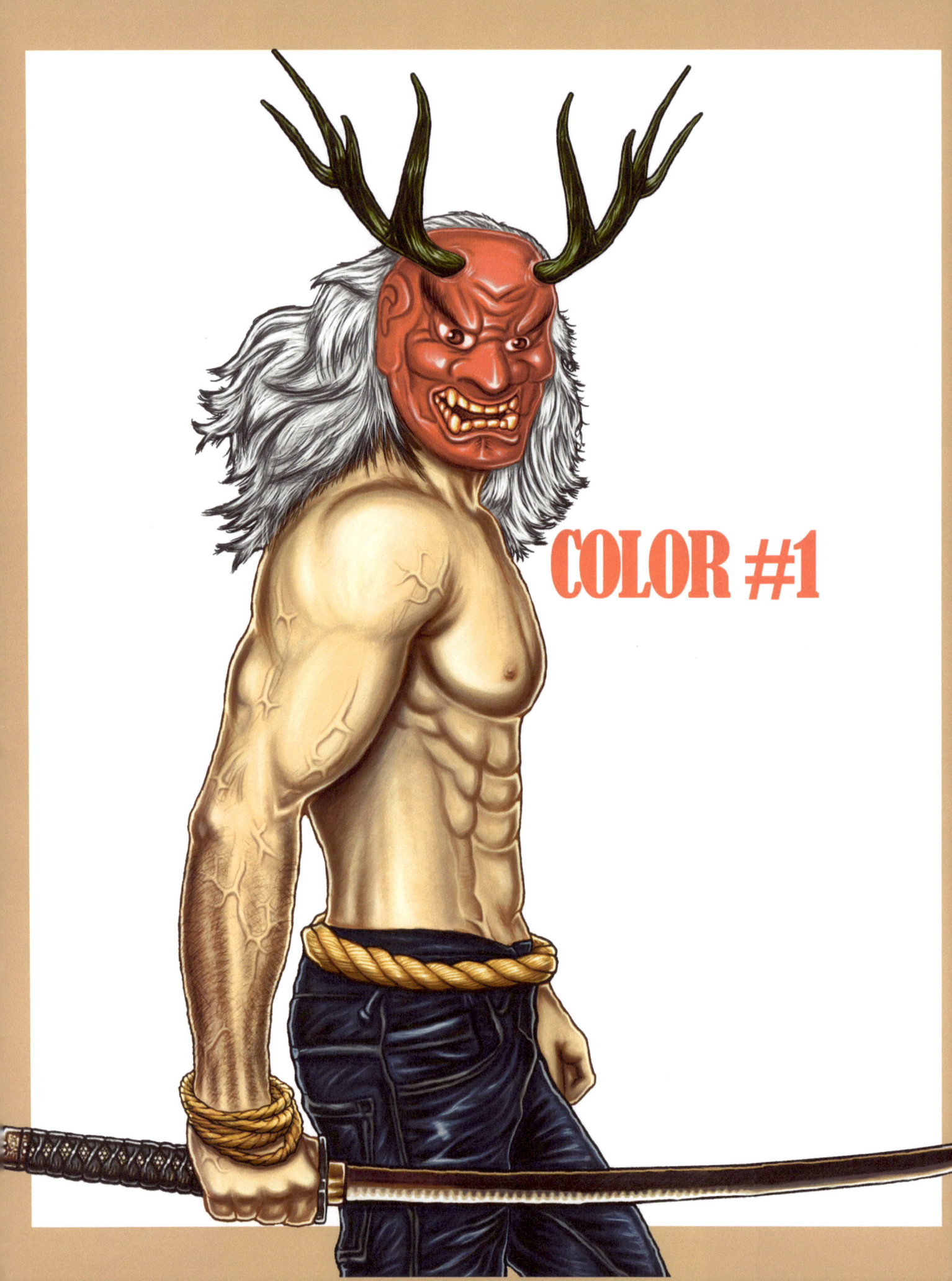

COLOR #1

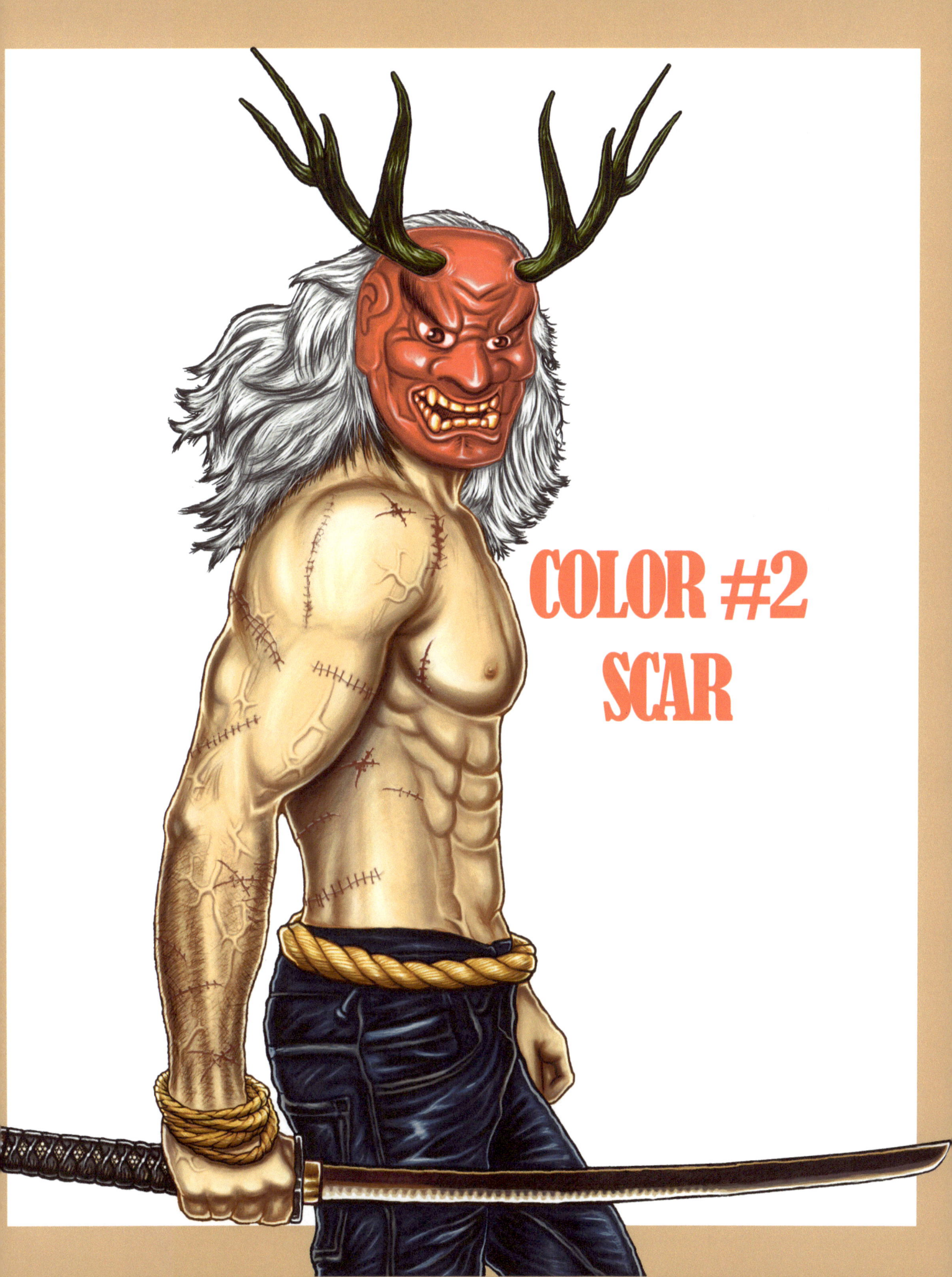

COLOR #2
SCAR

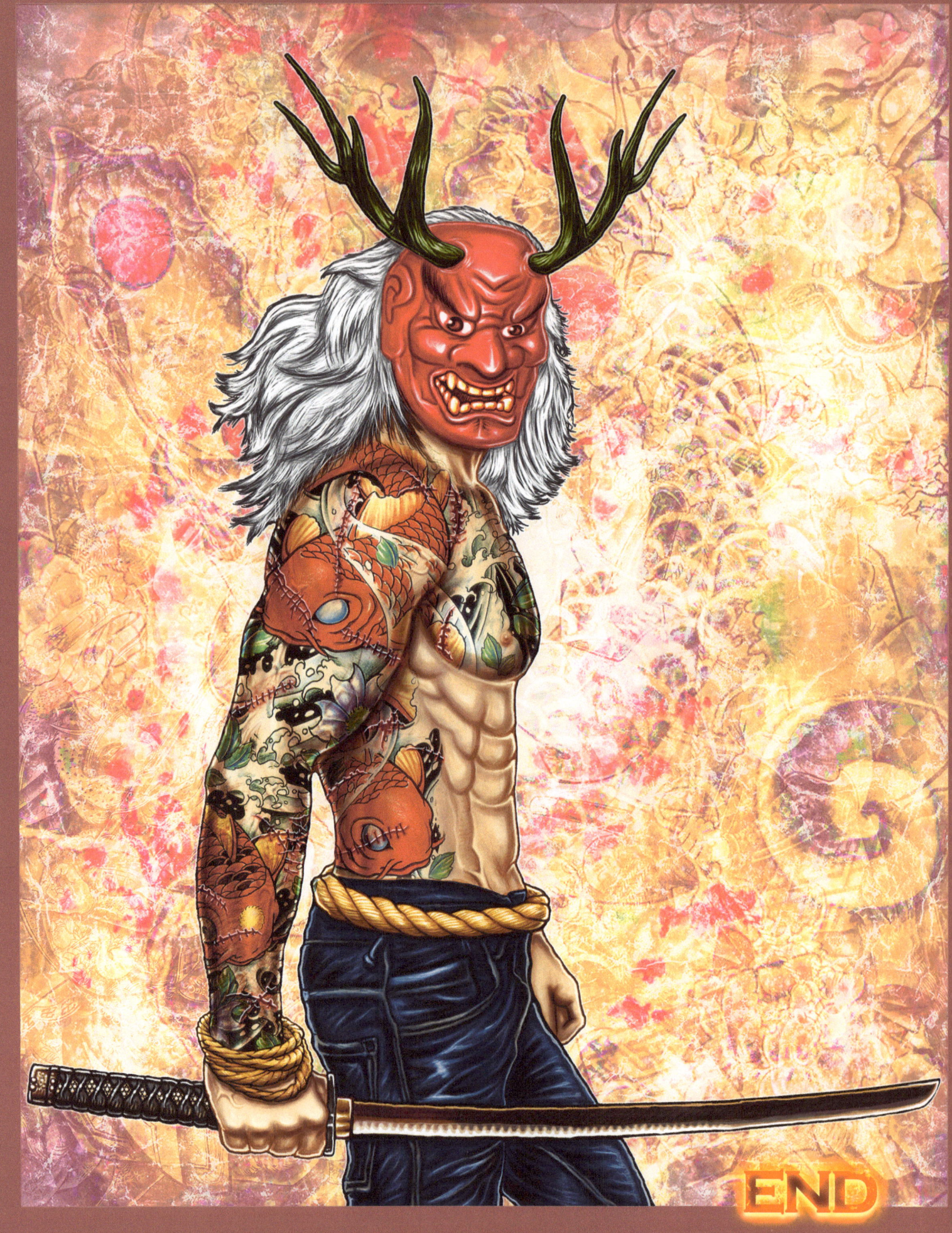

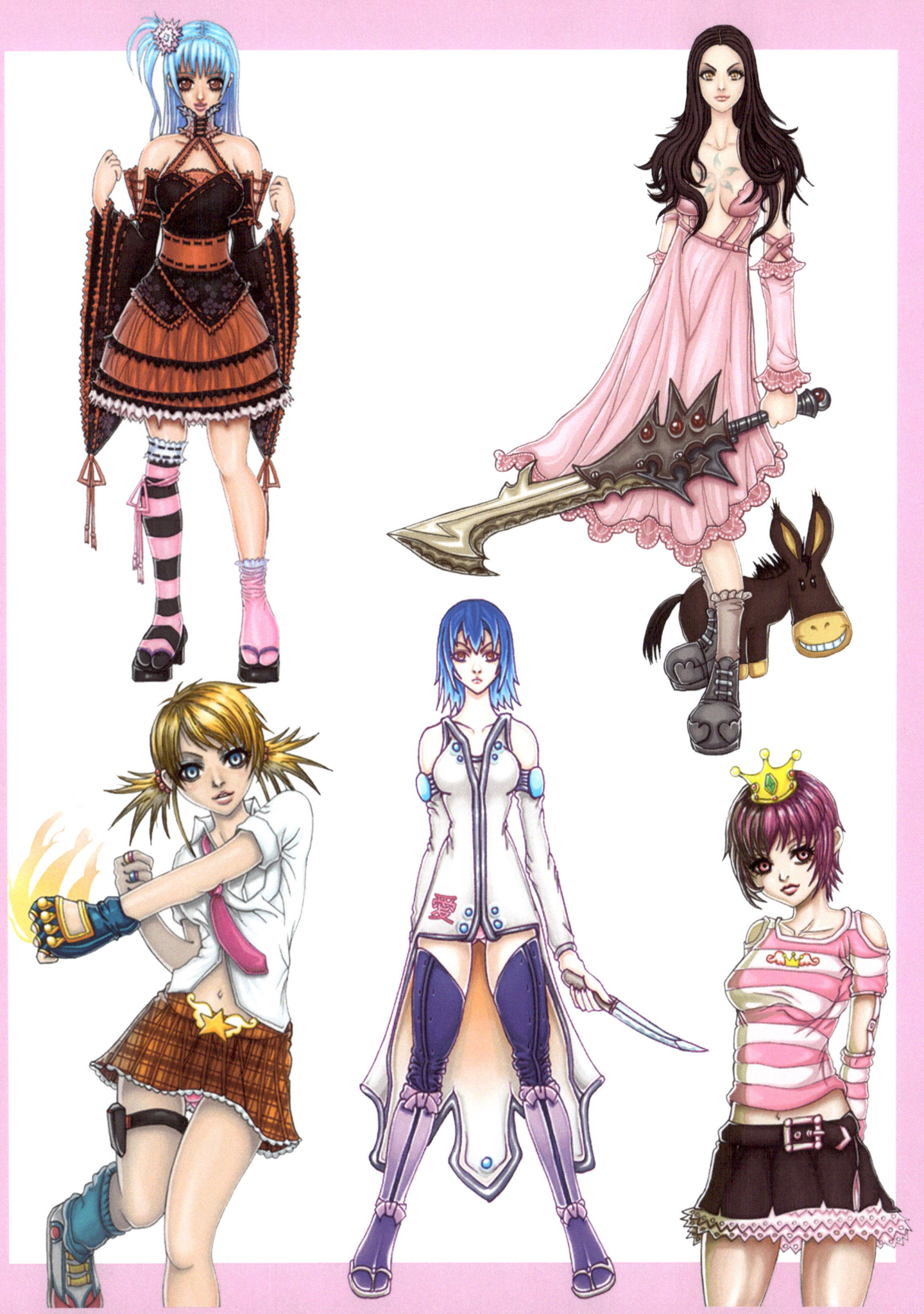

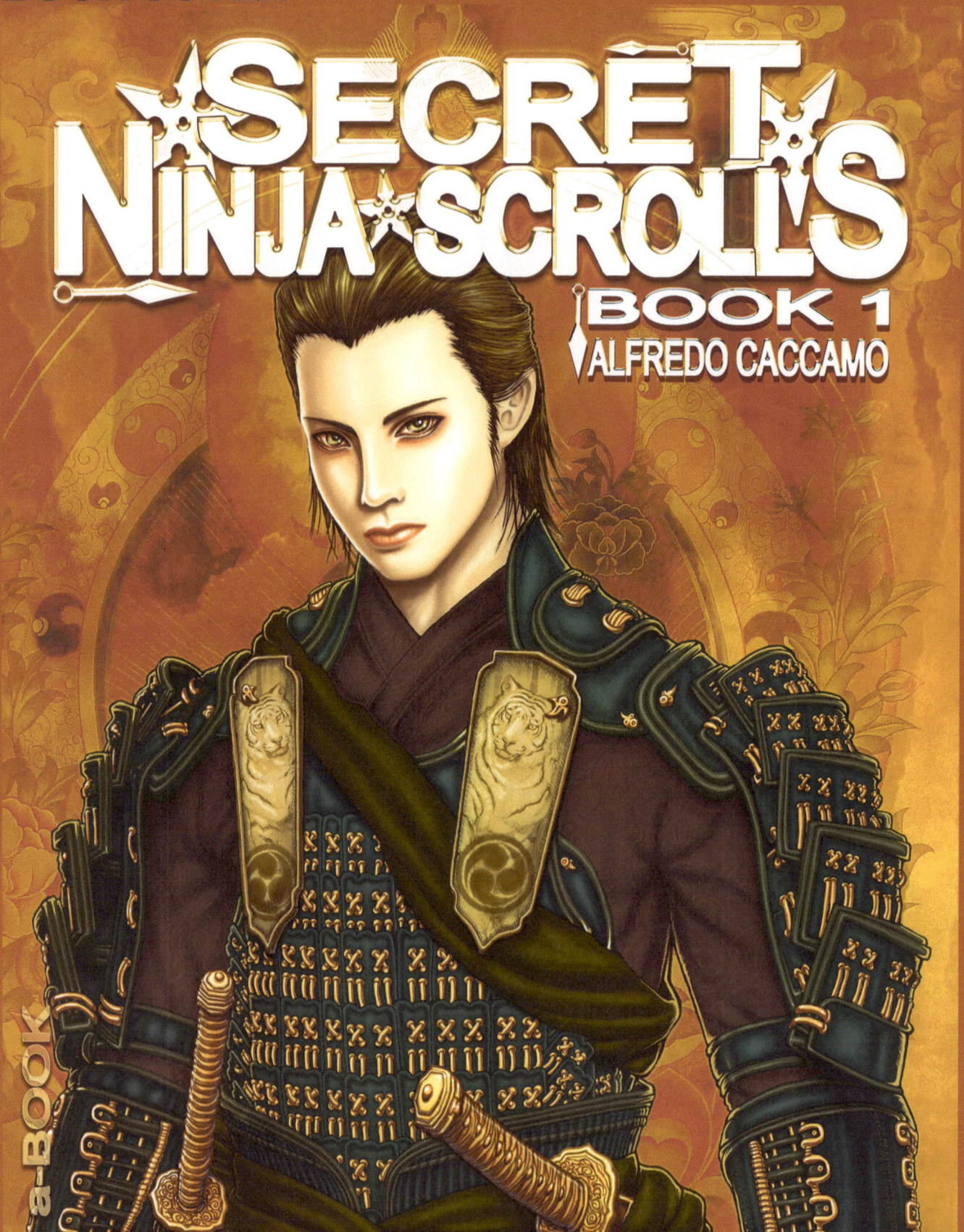

SECRET NINJA SCROLLS

BOOK 1

ALFREDO CACCAMO

a-BOOK

GOLD EDITION of I ROTOLI SEGRETI DEI NINJA #1

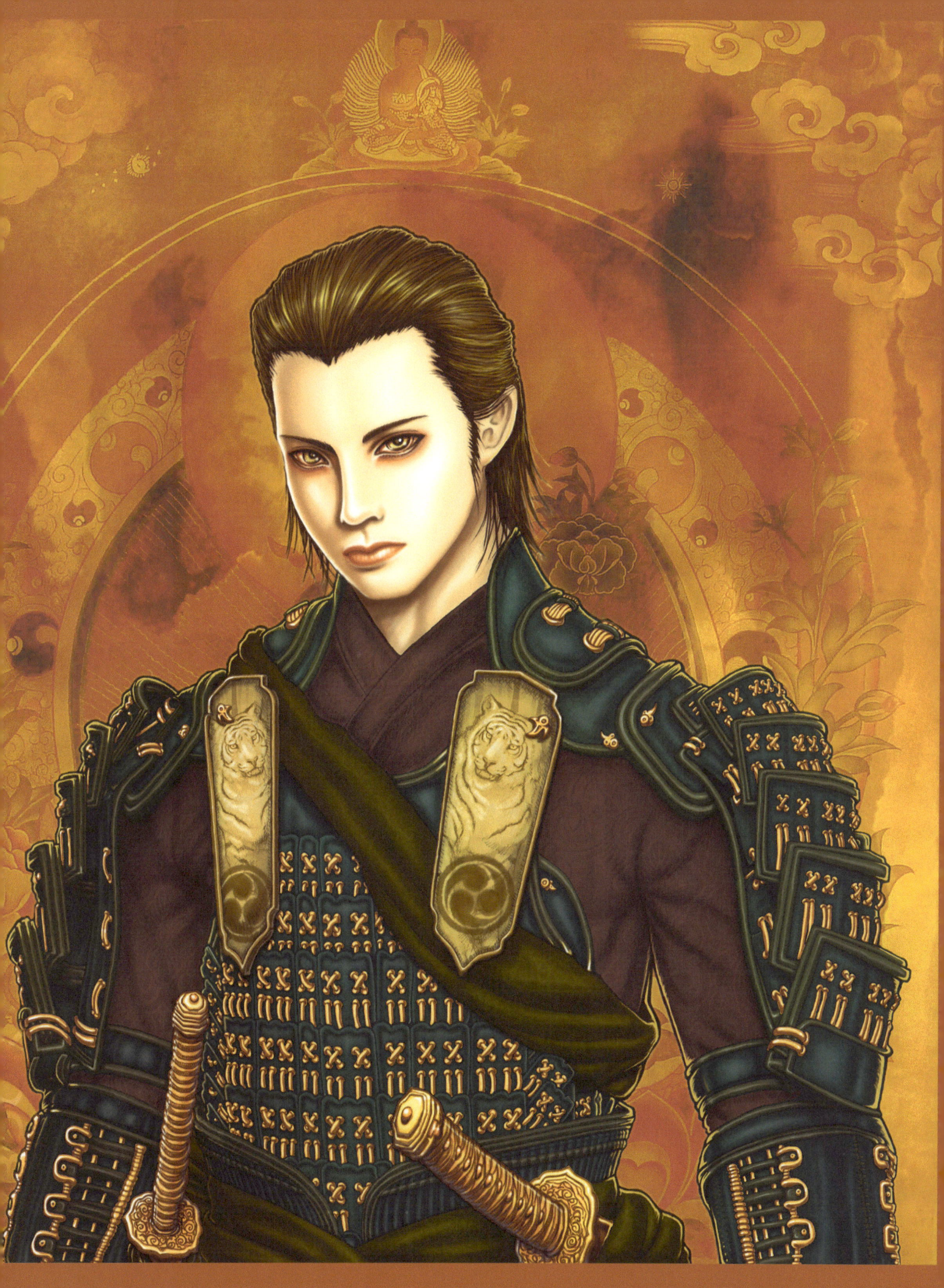

I Rotoli Segreti dei Ninja

ALFREDO CACCAMO

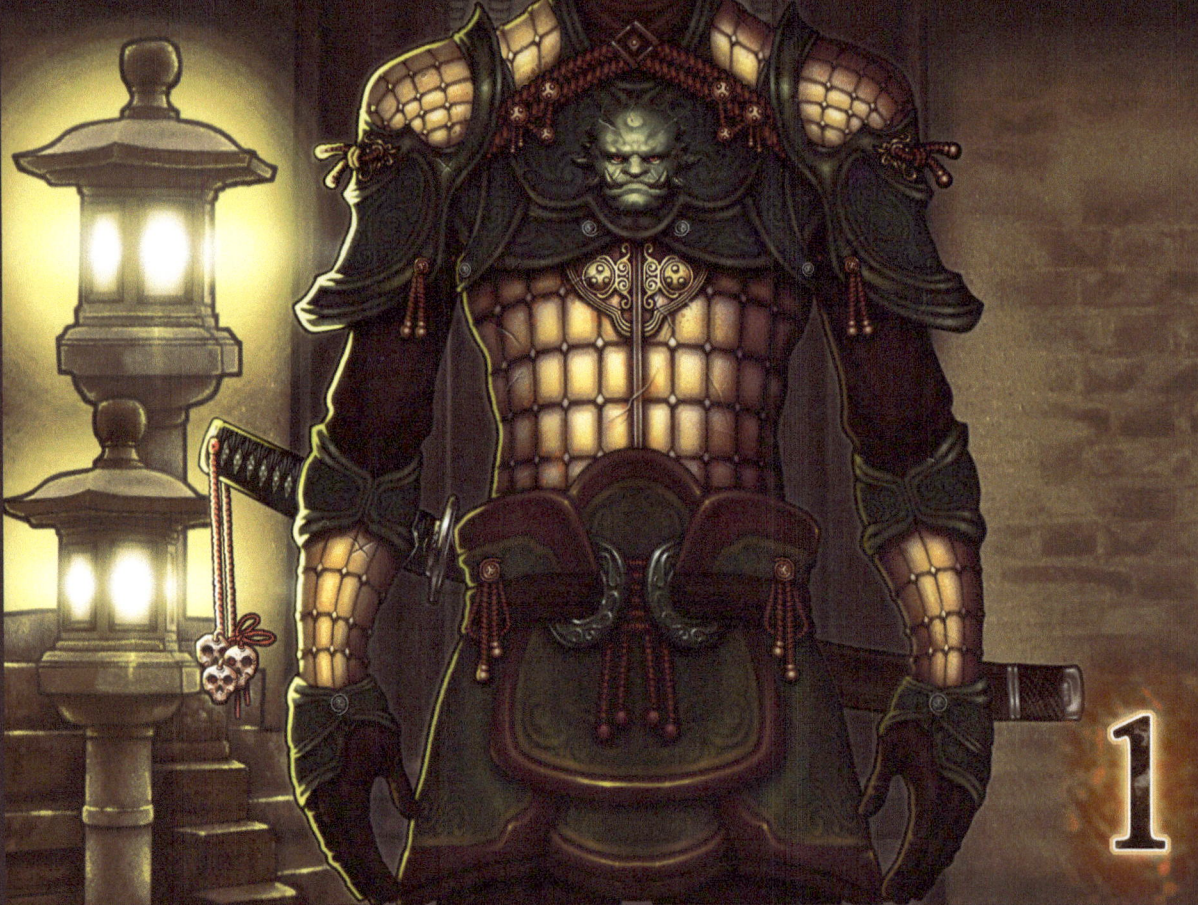

1

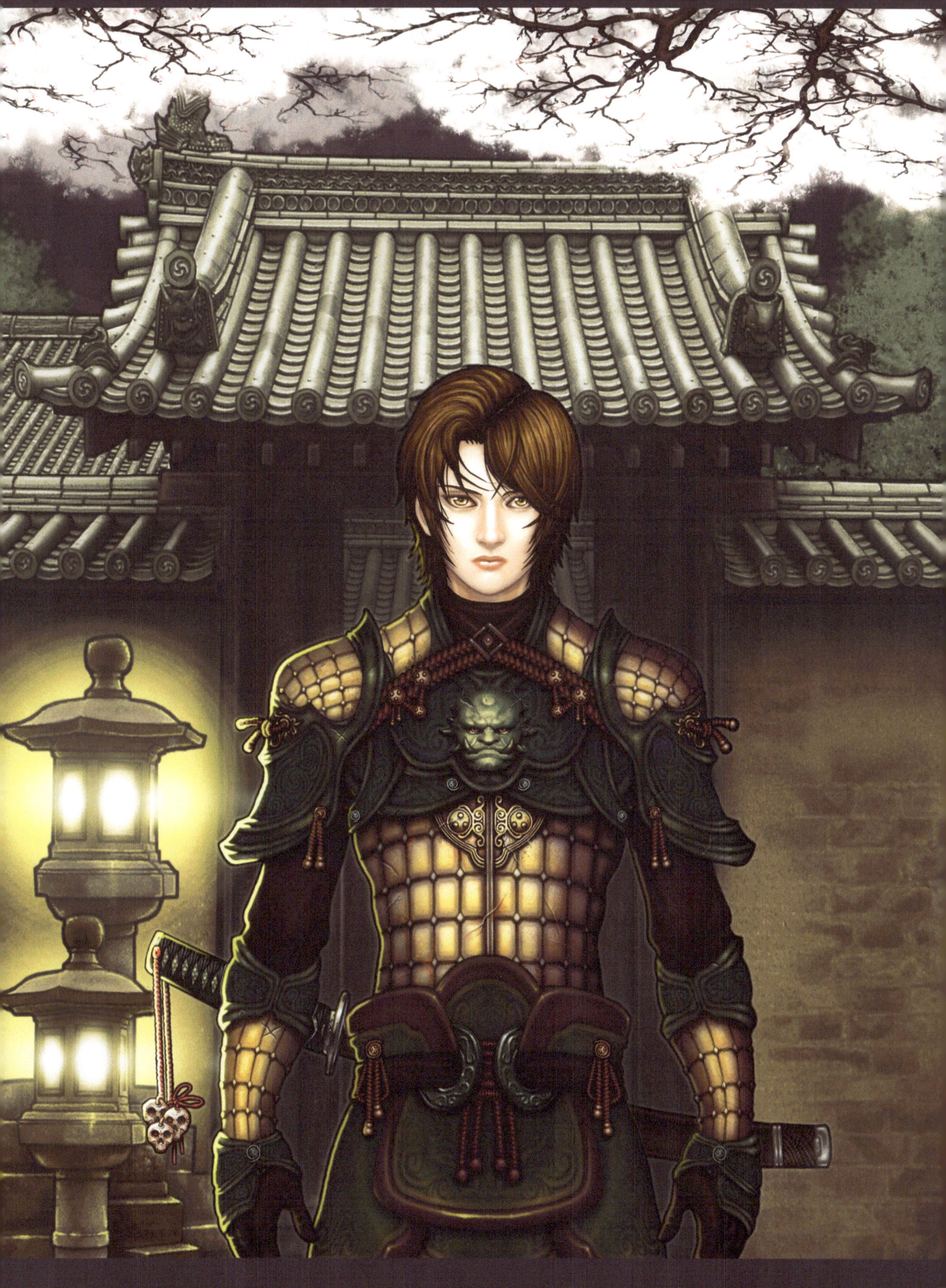

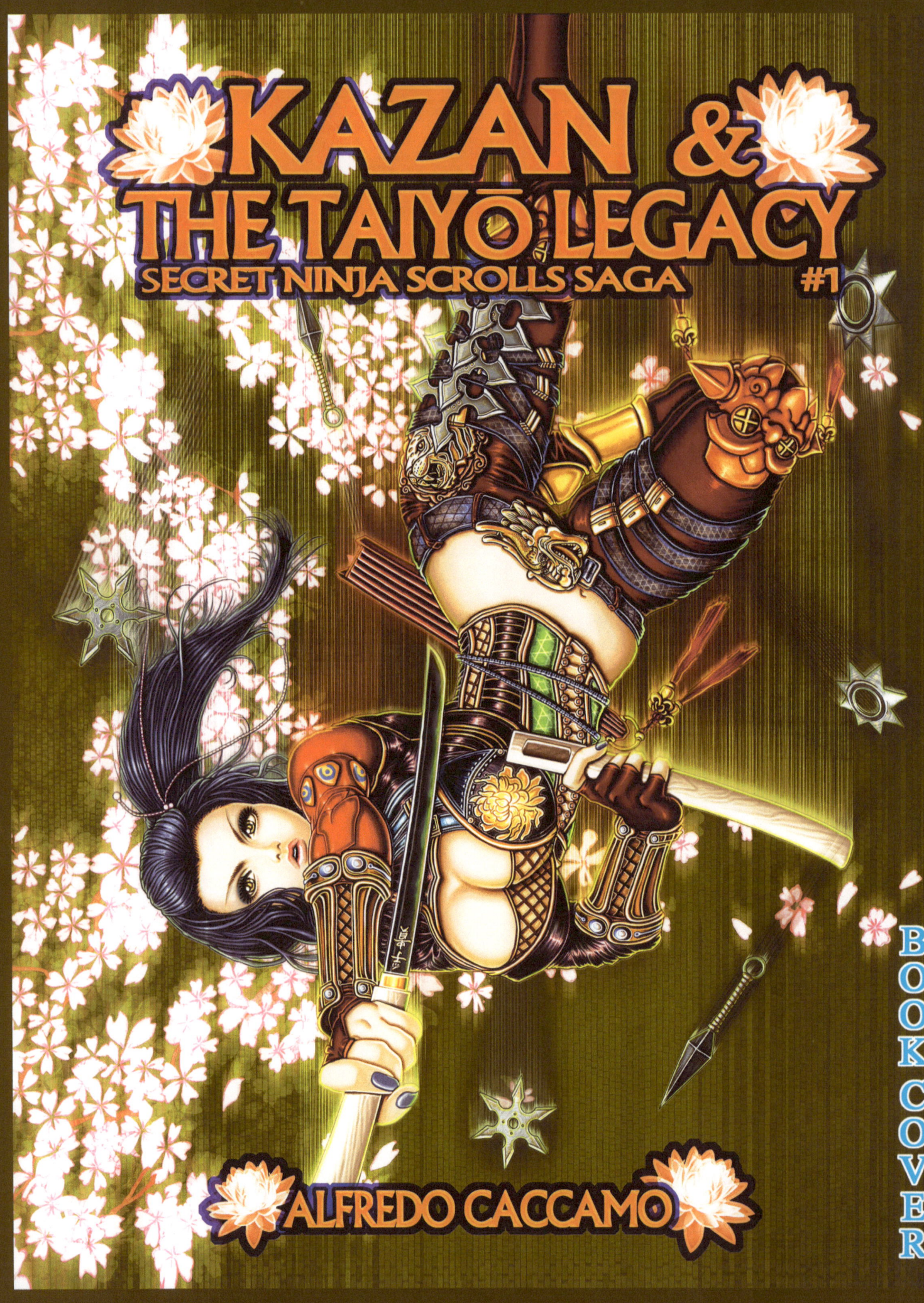

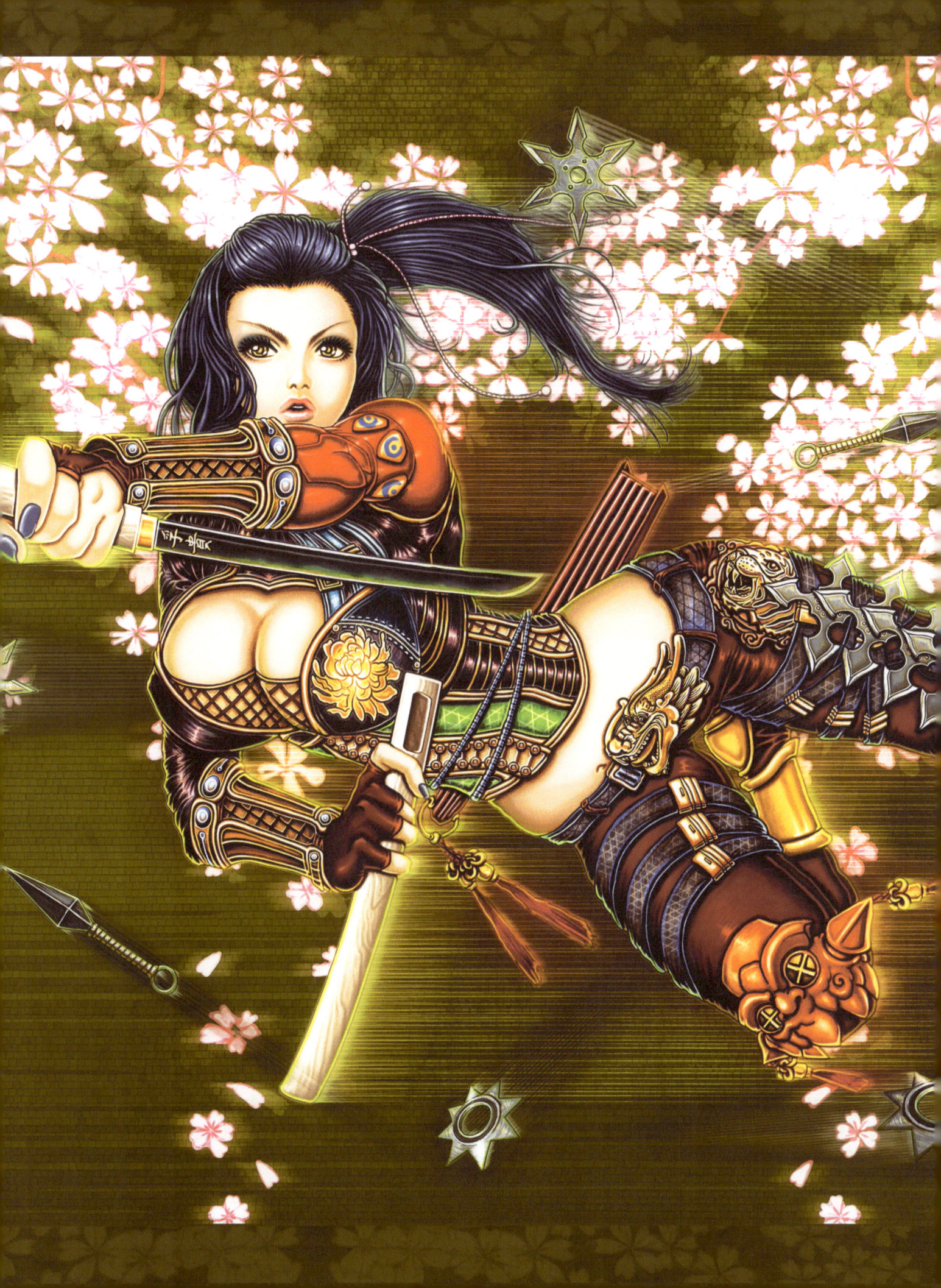

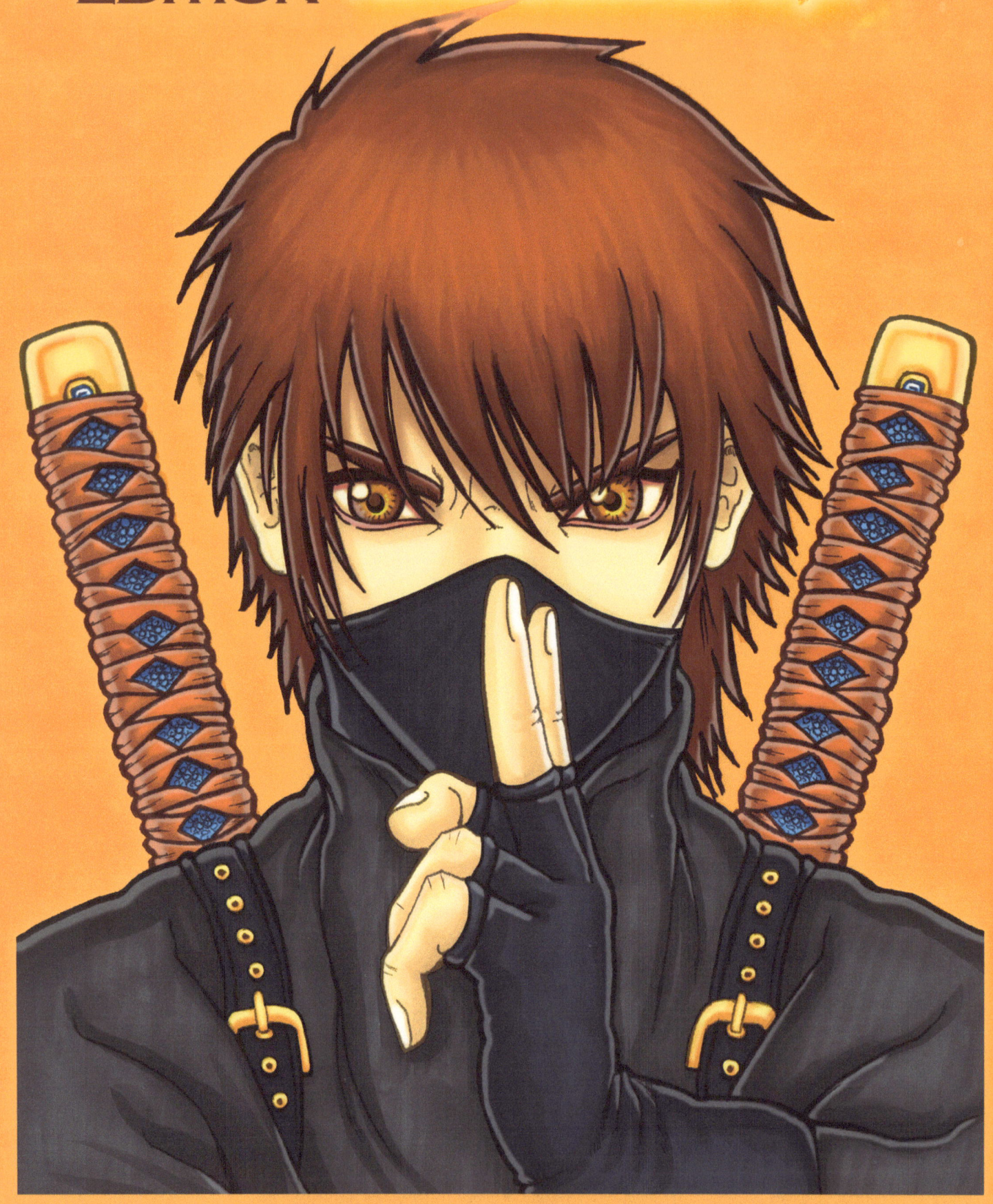

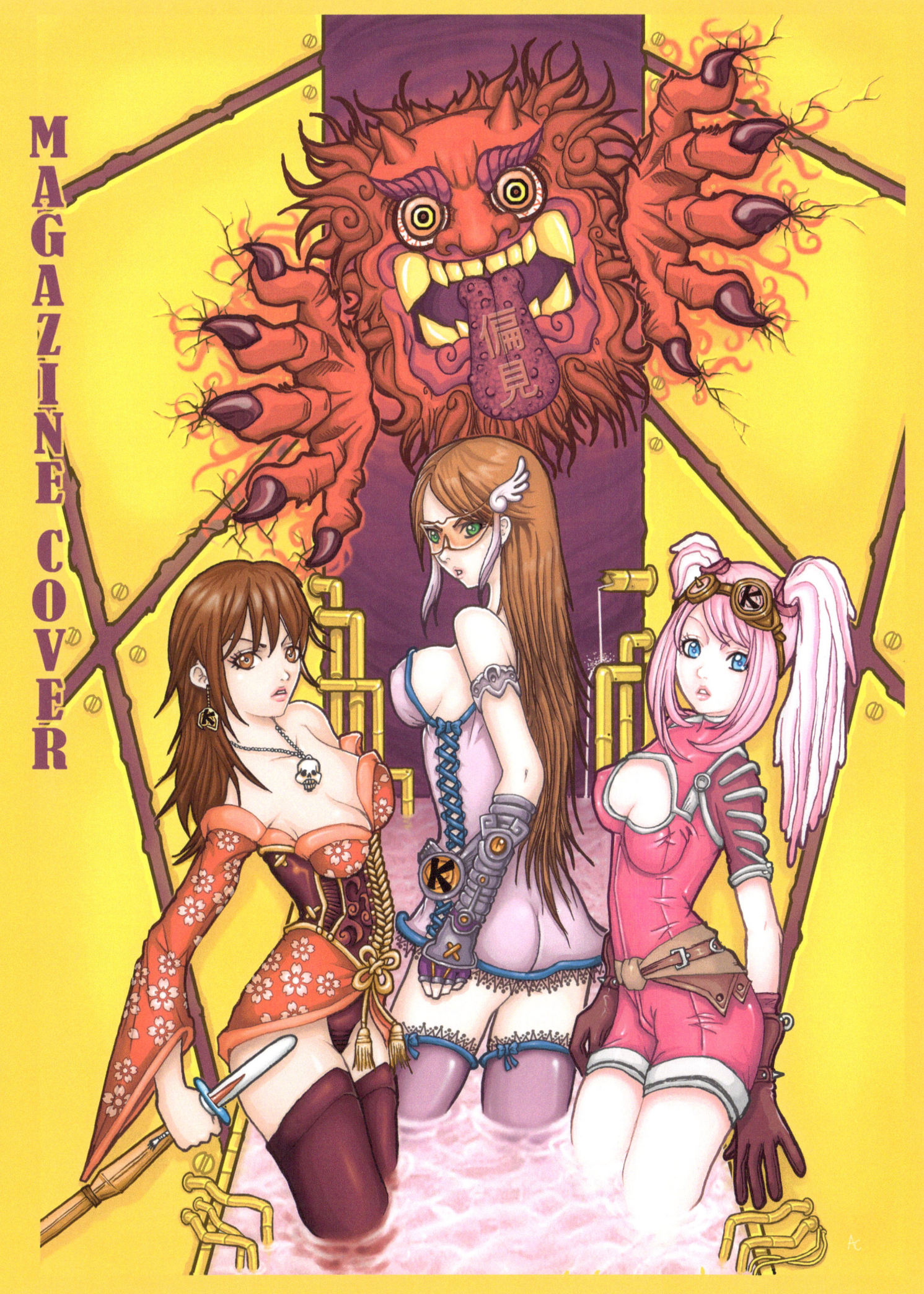

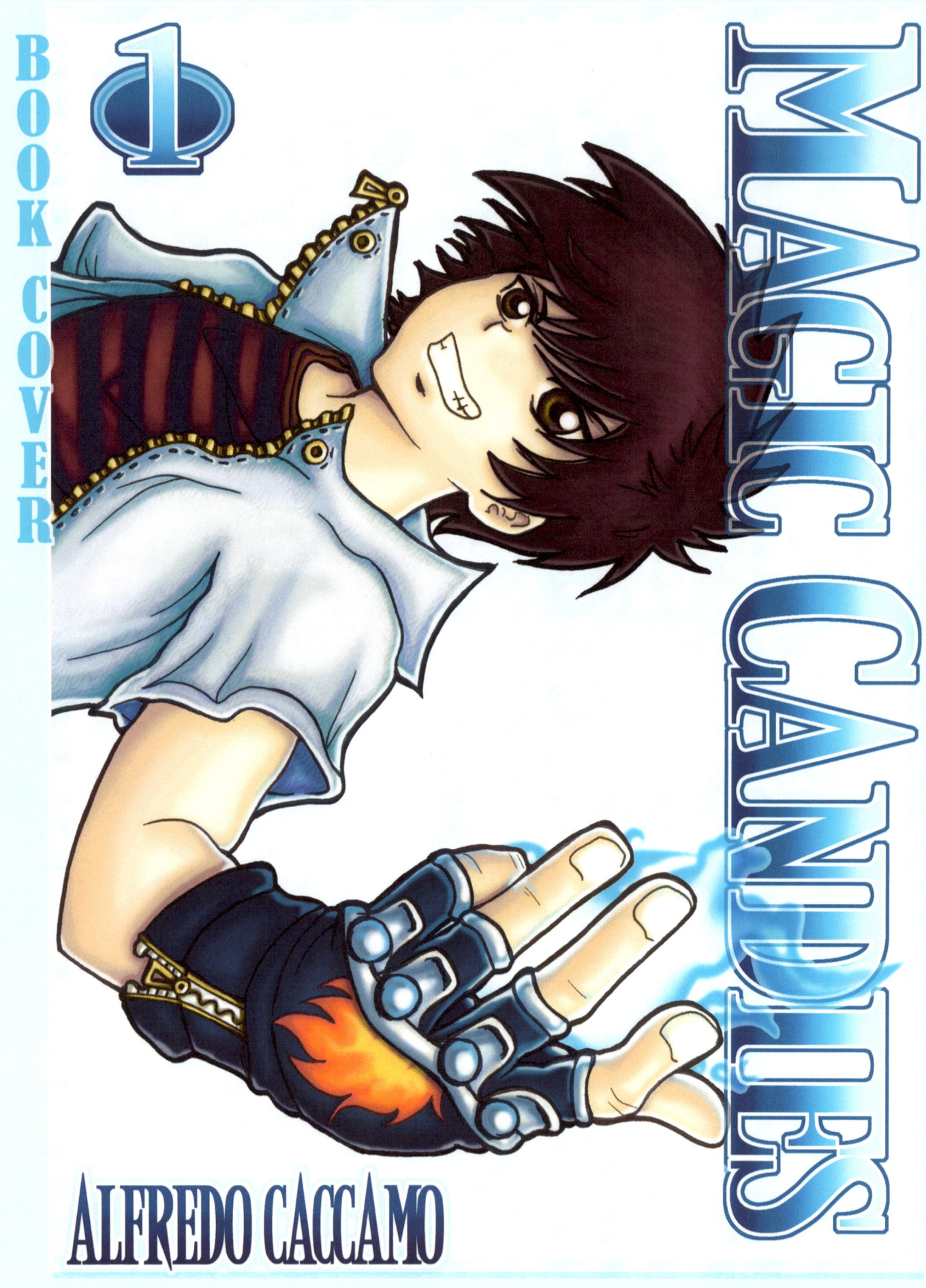

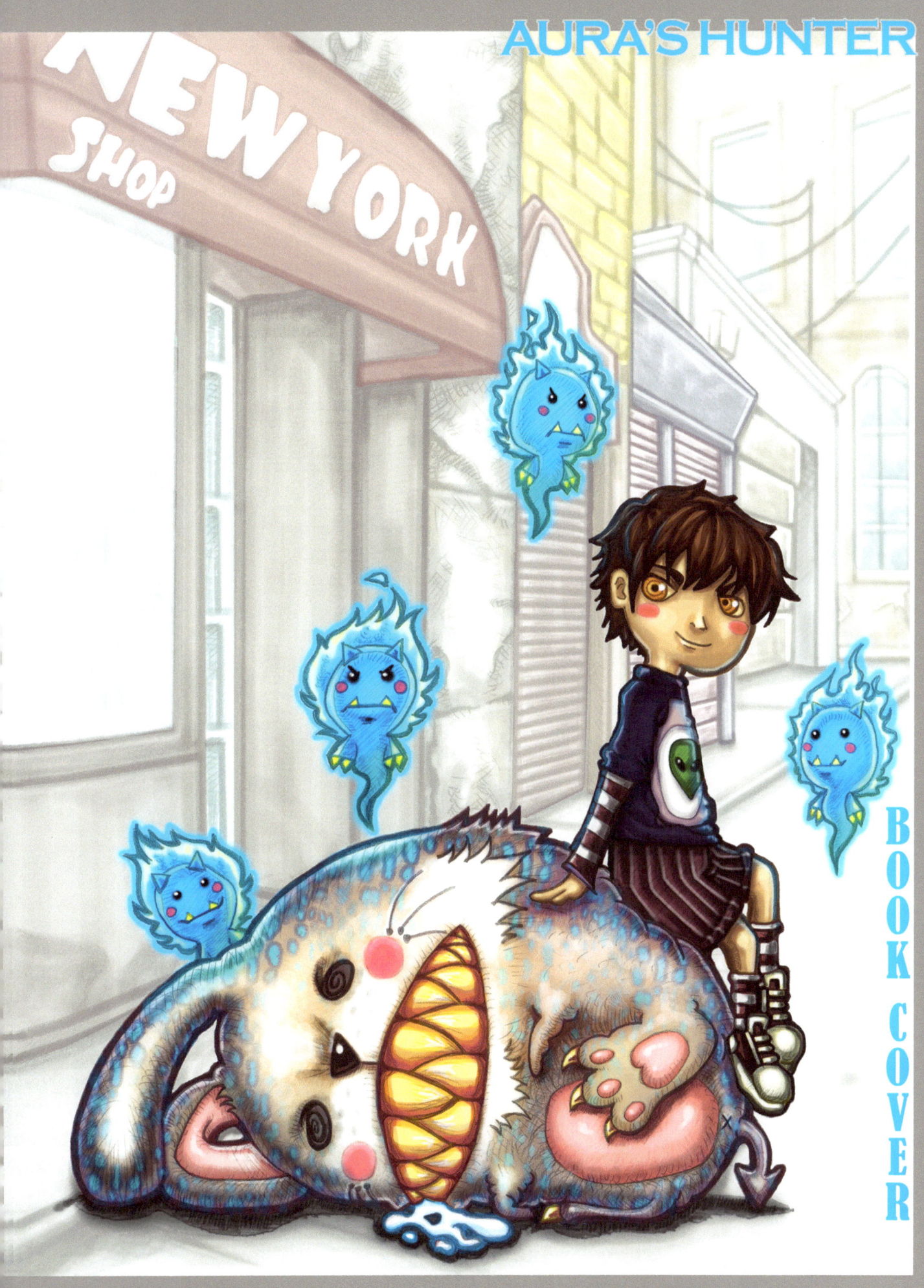

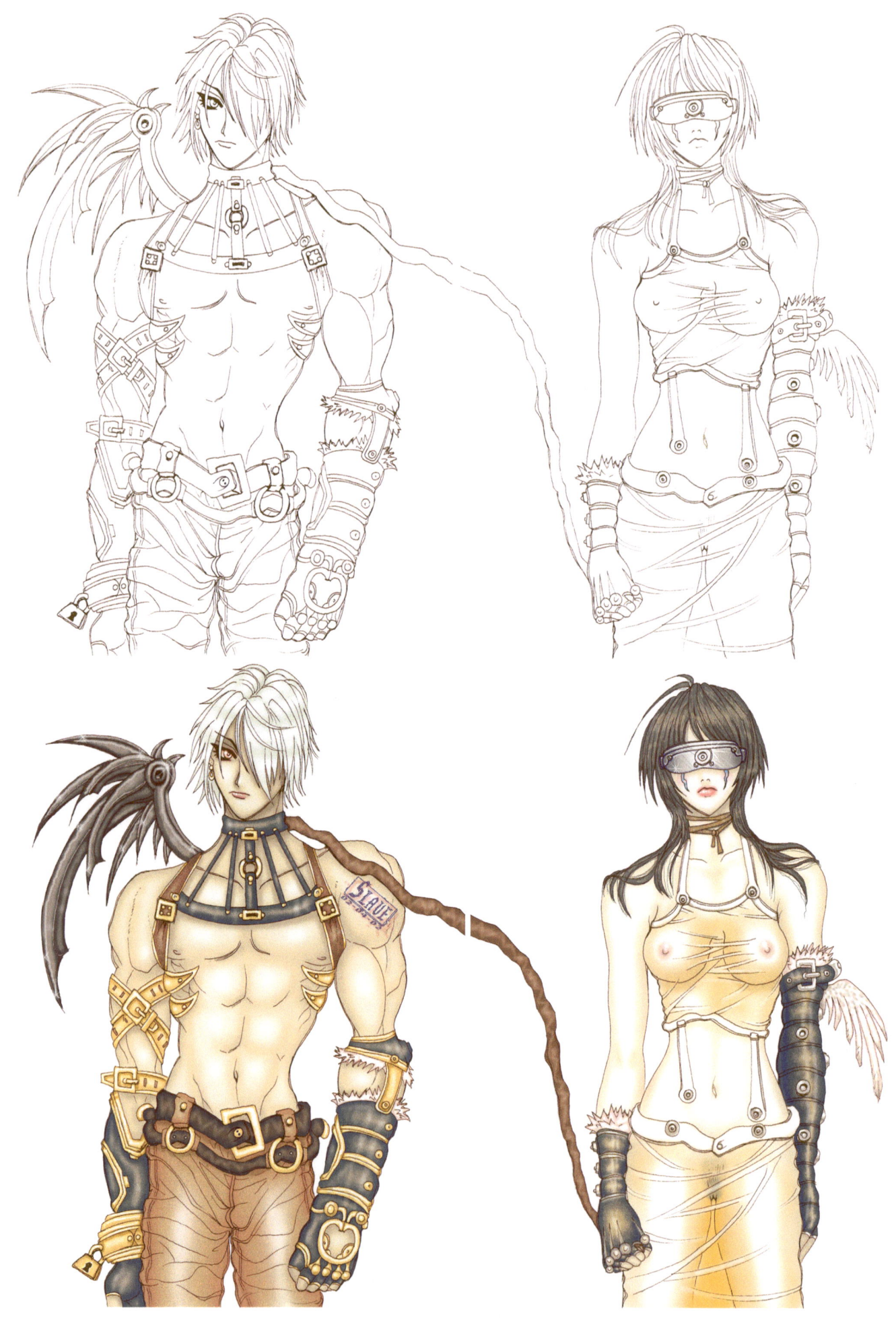

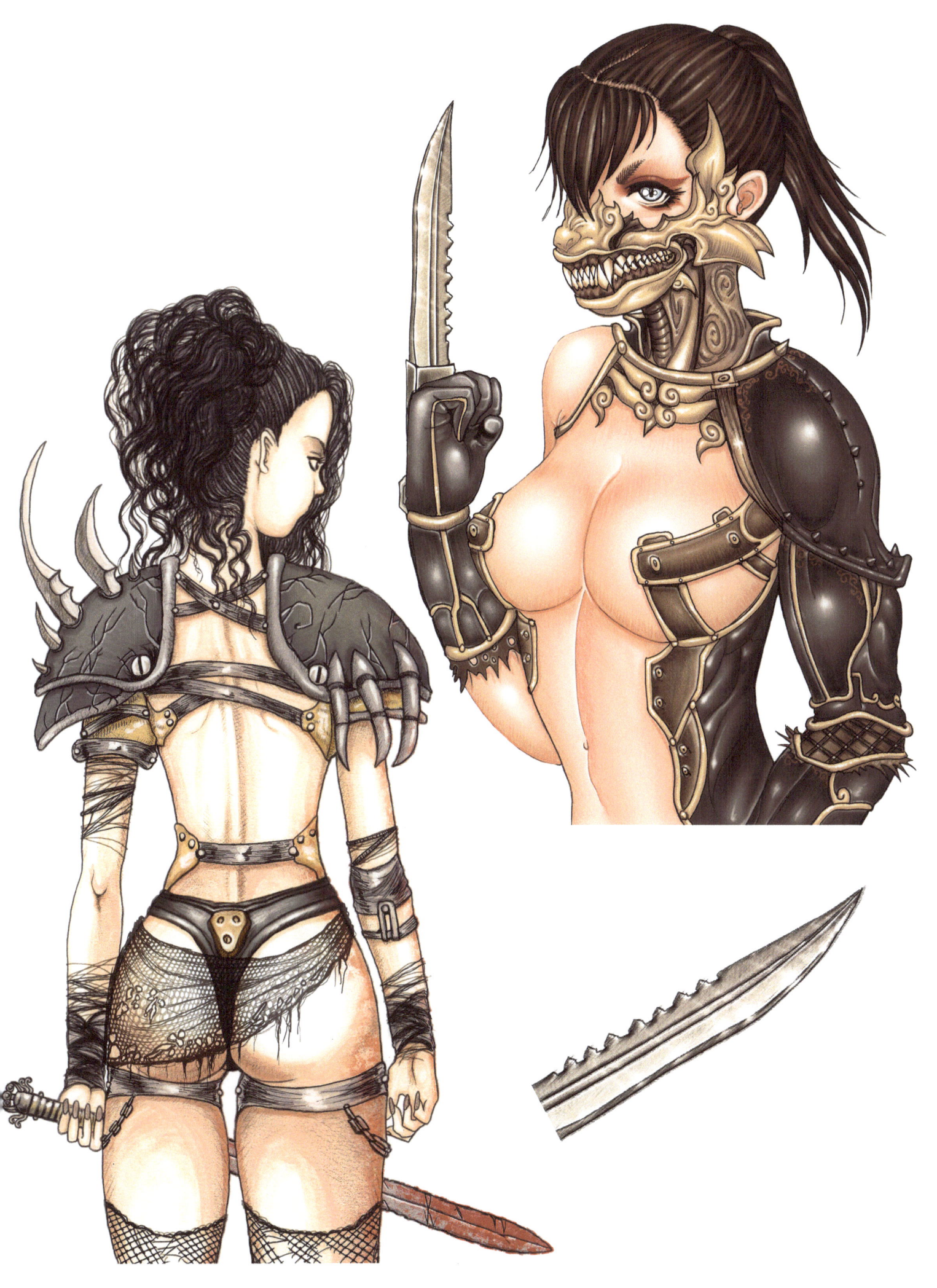

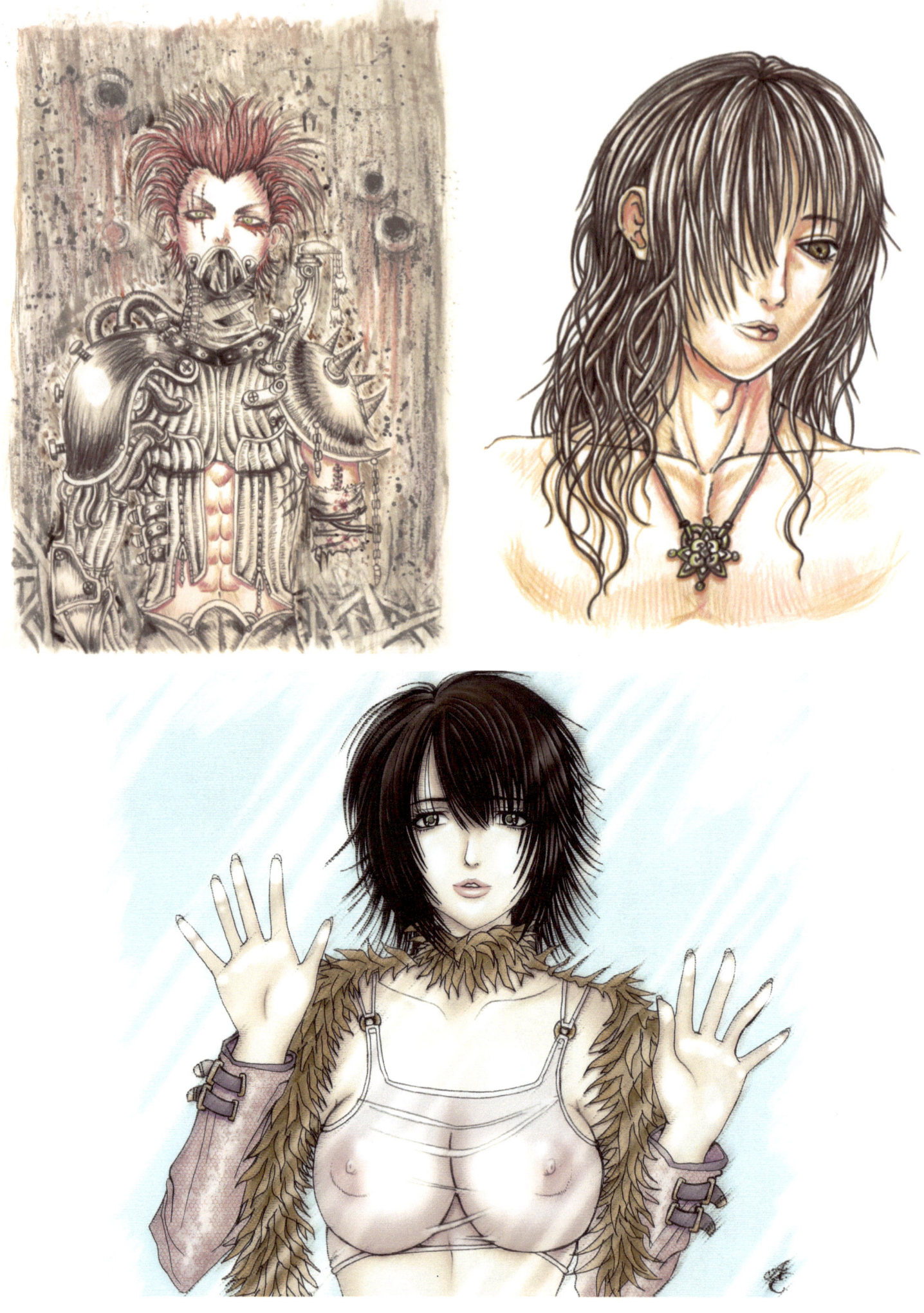

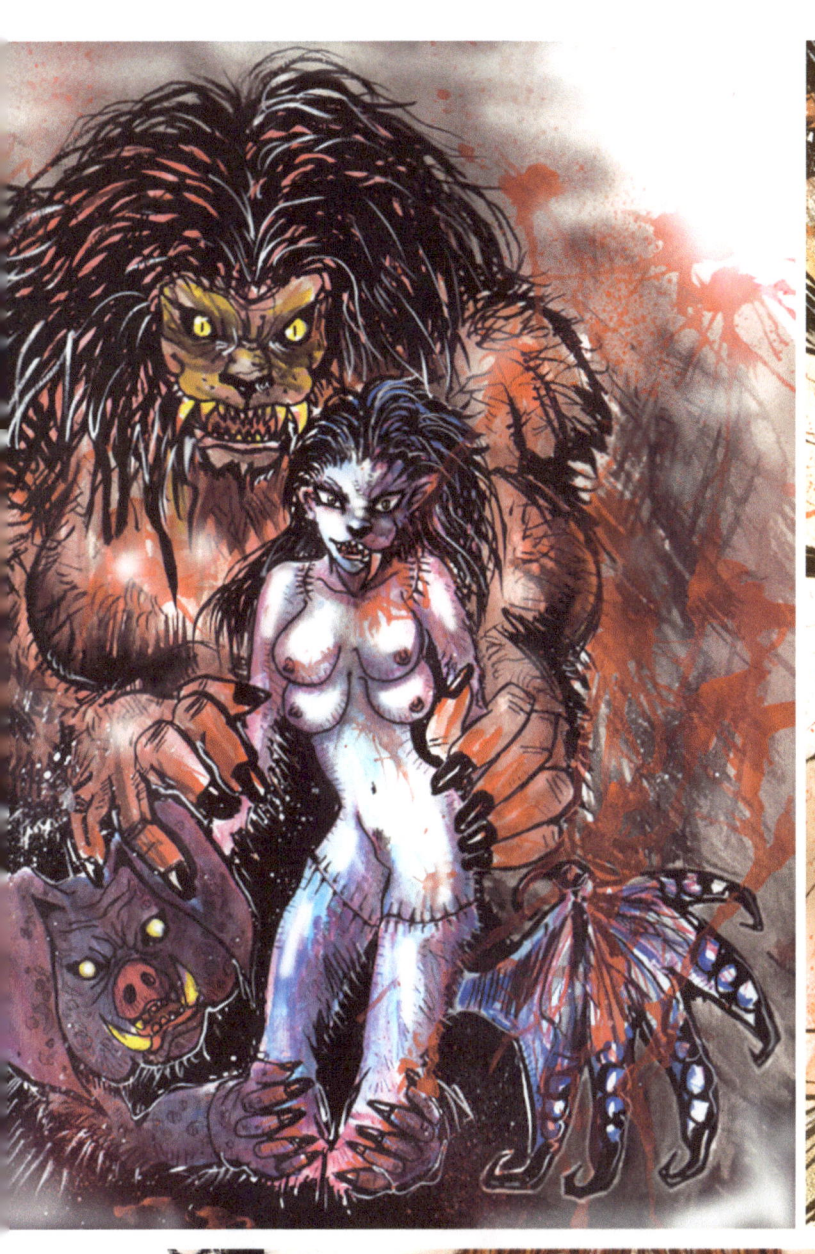

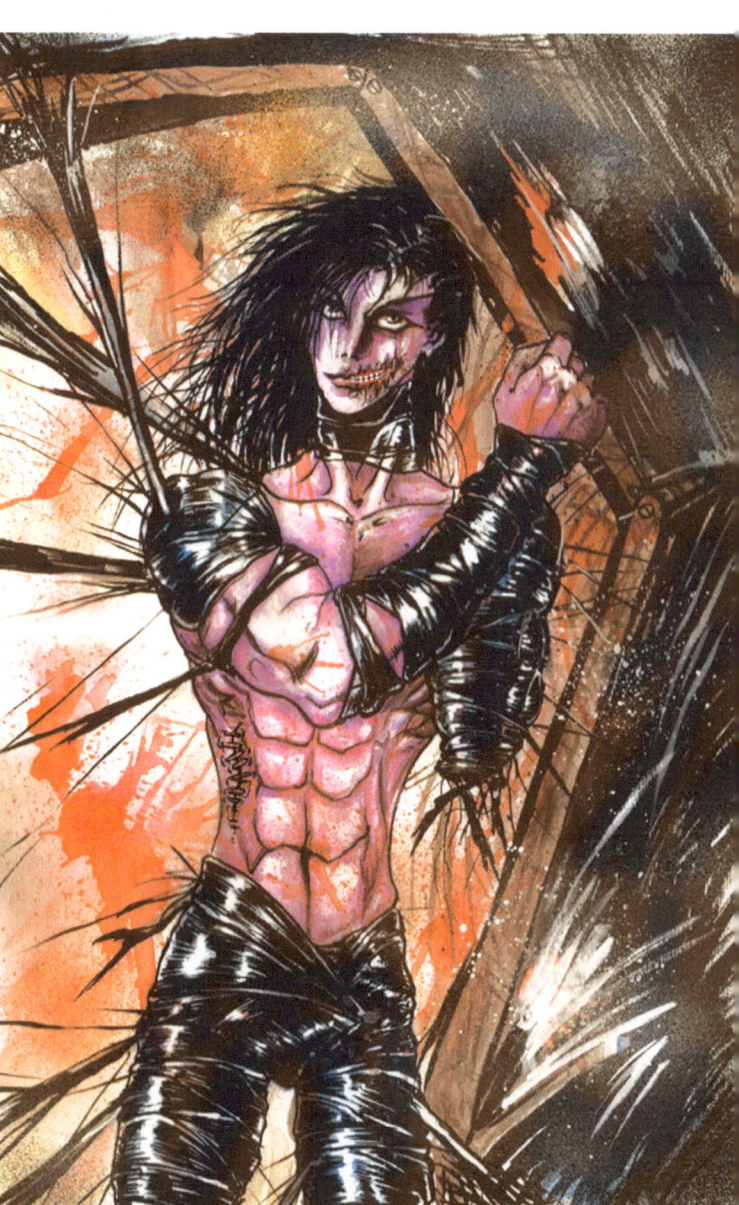

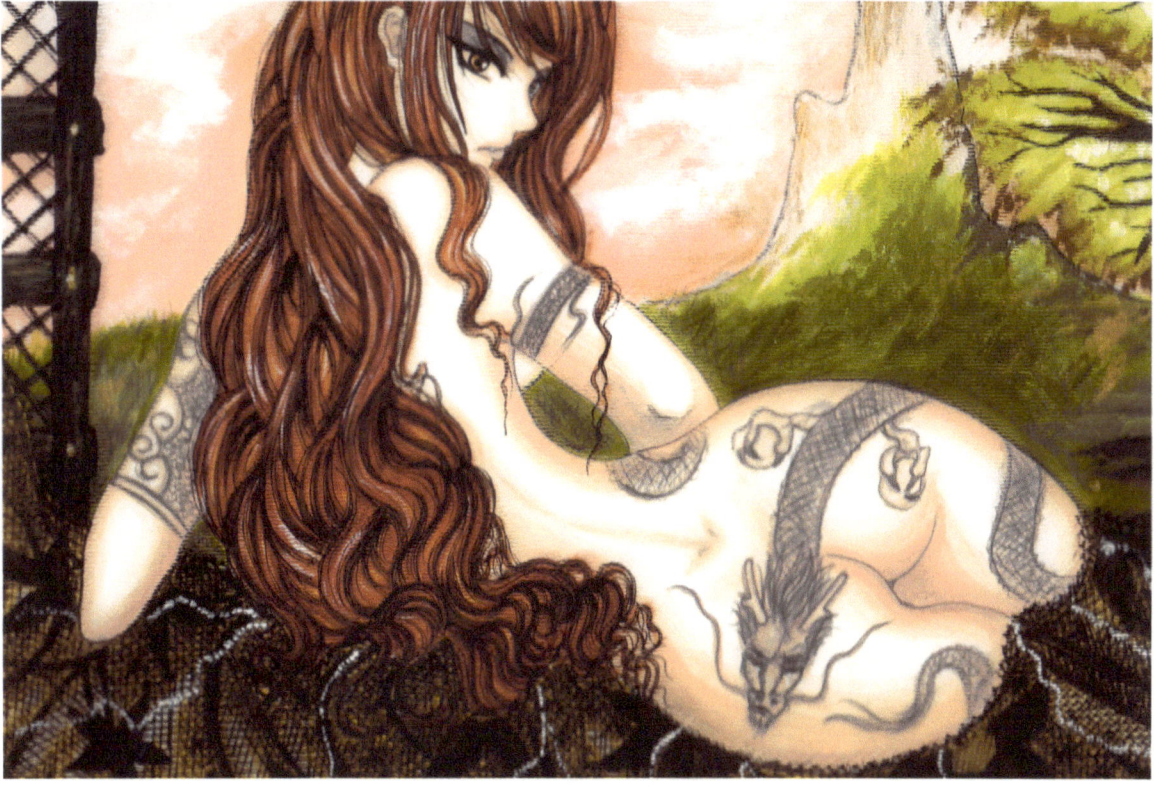

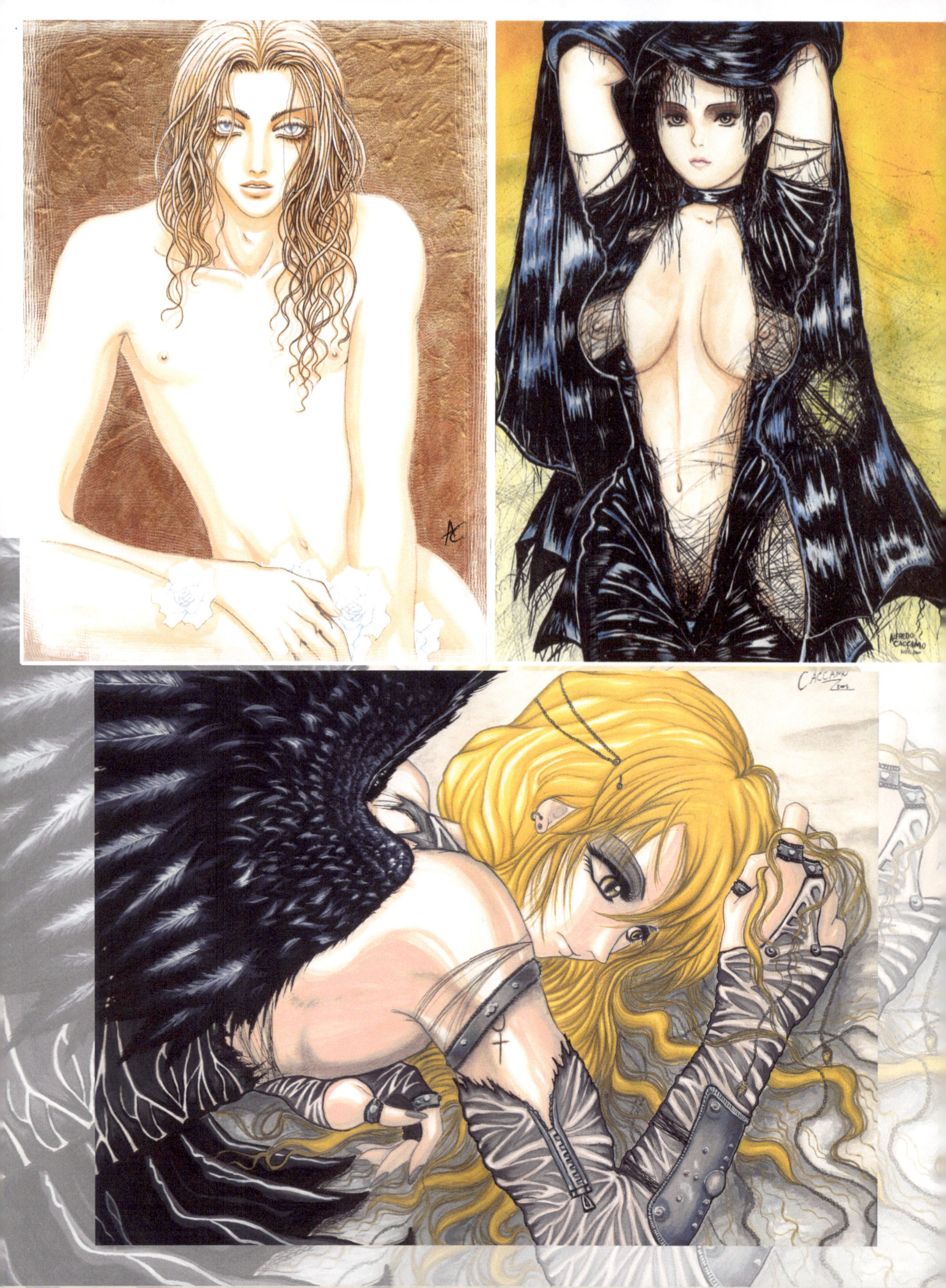

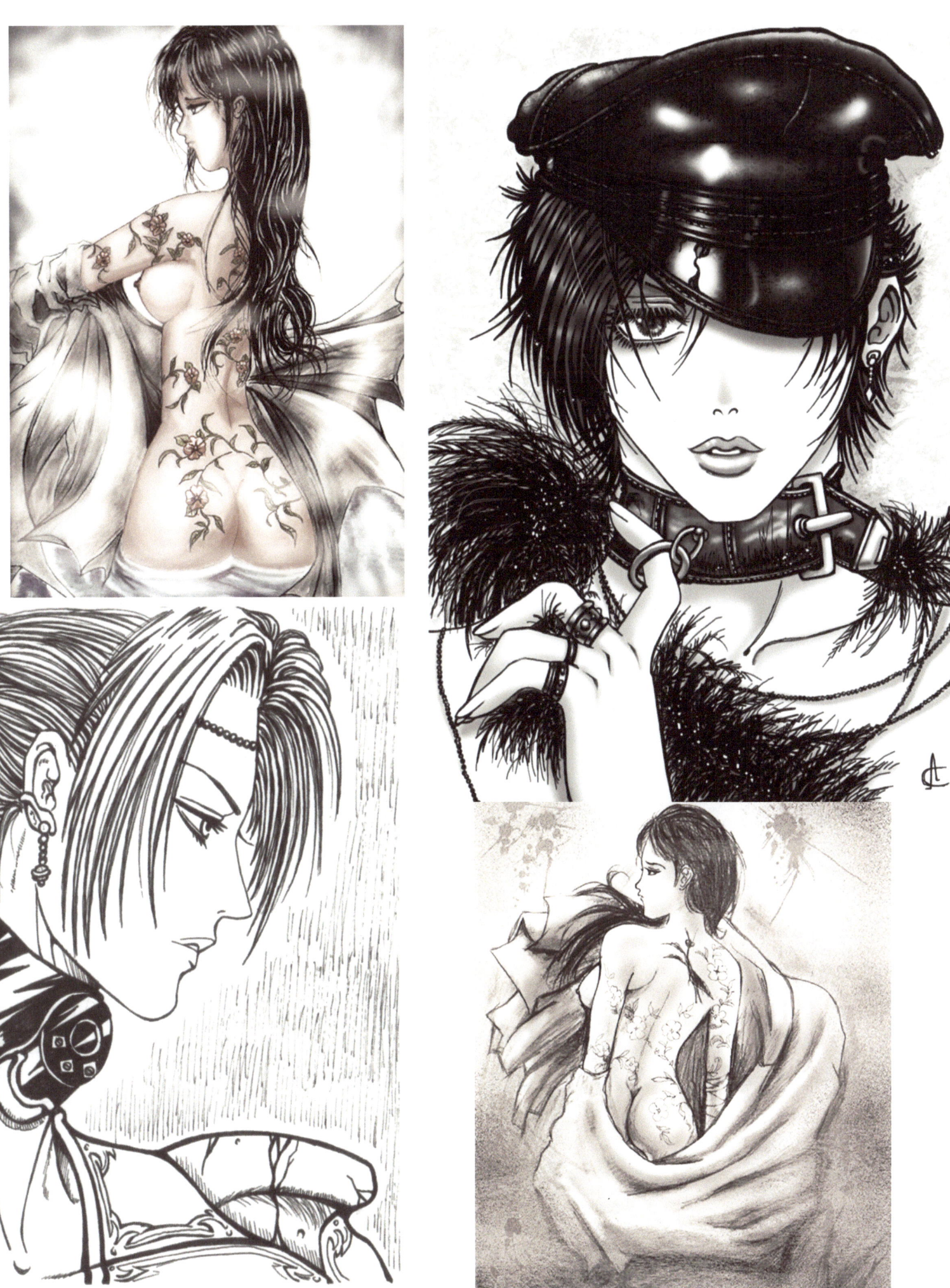

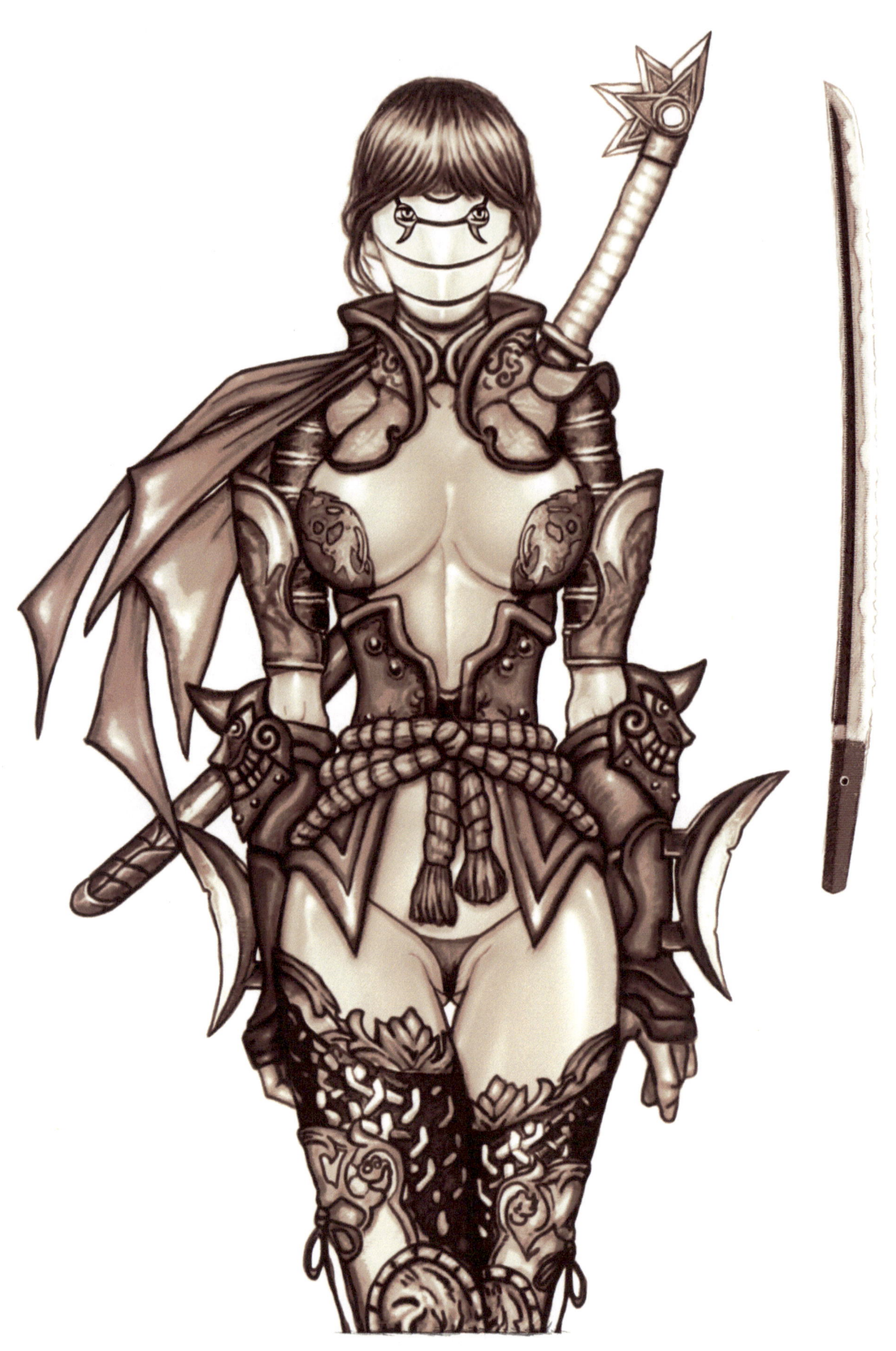

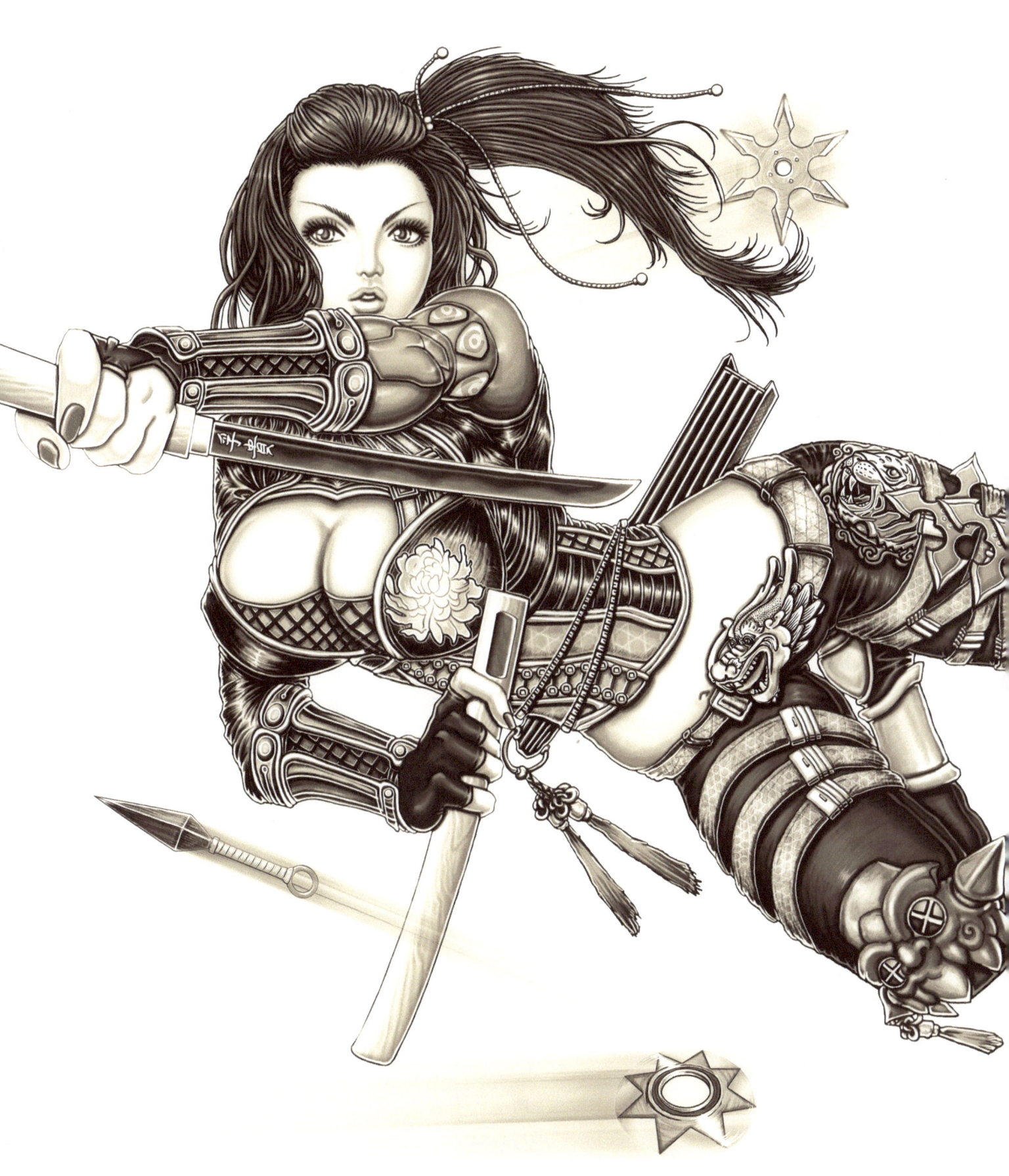

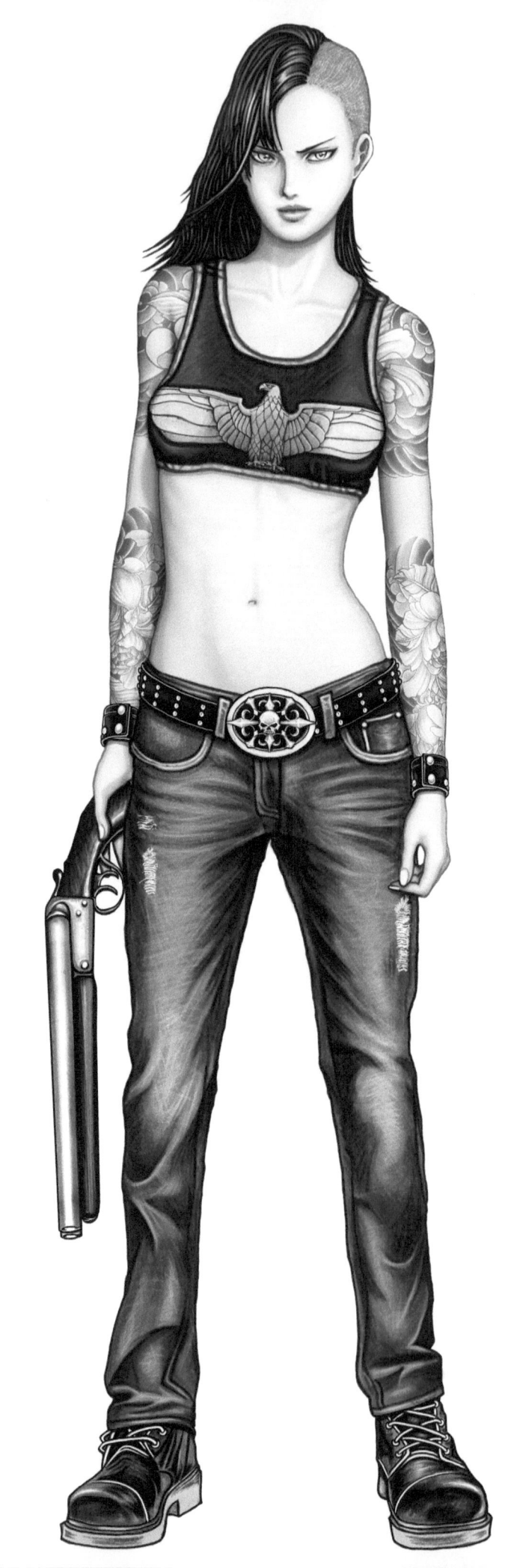

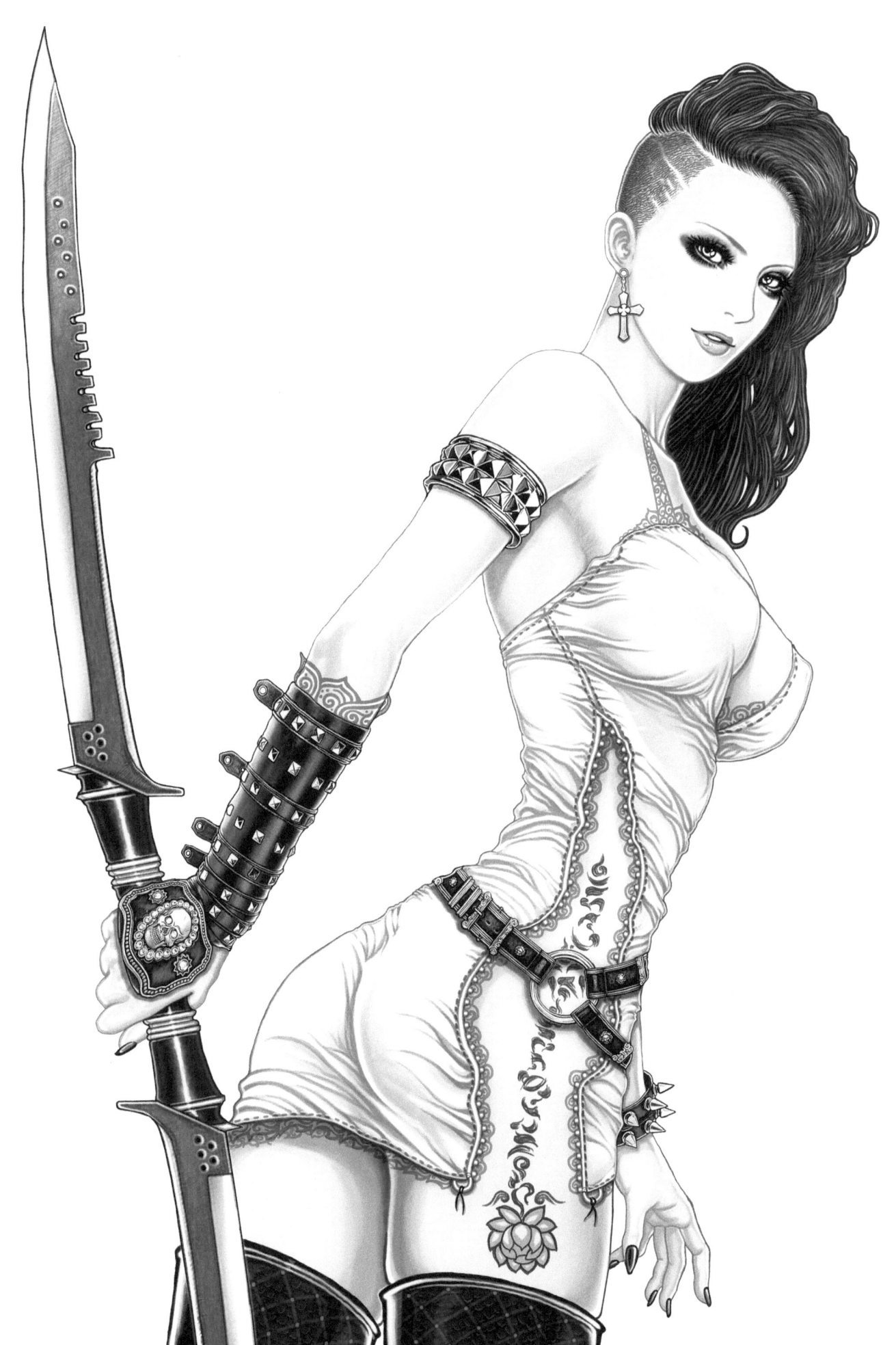

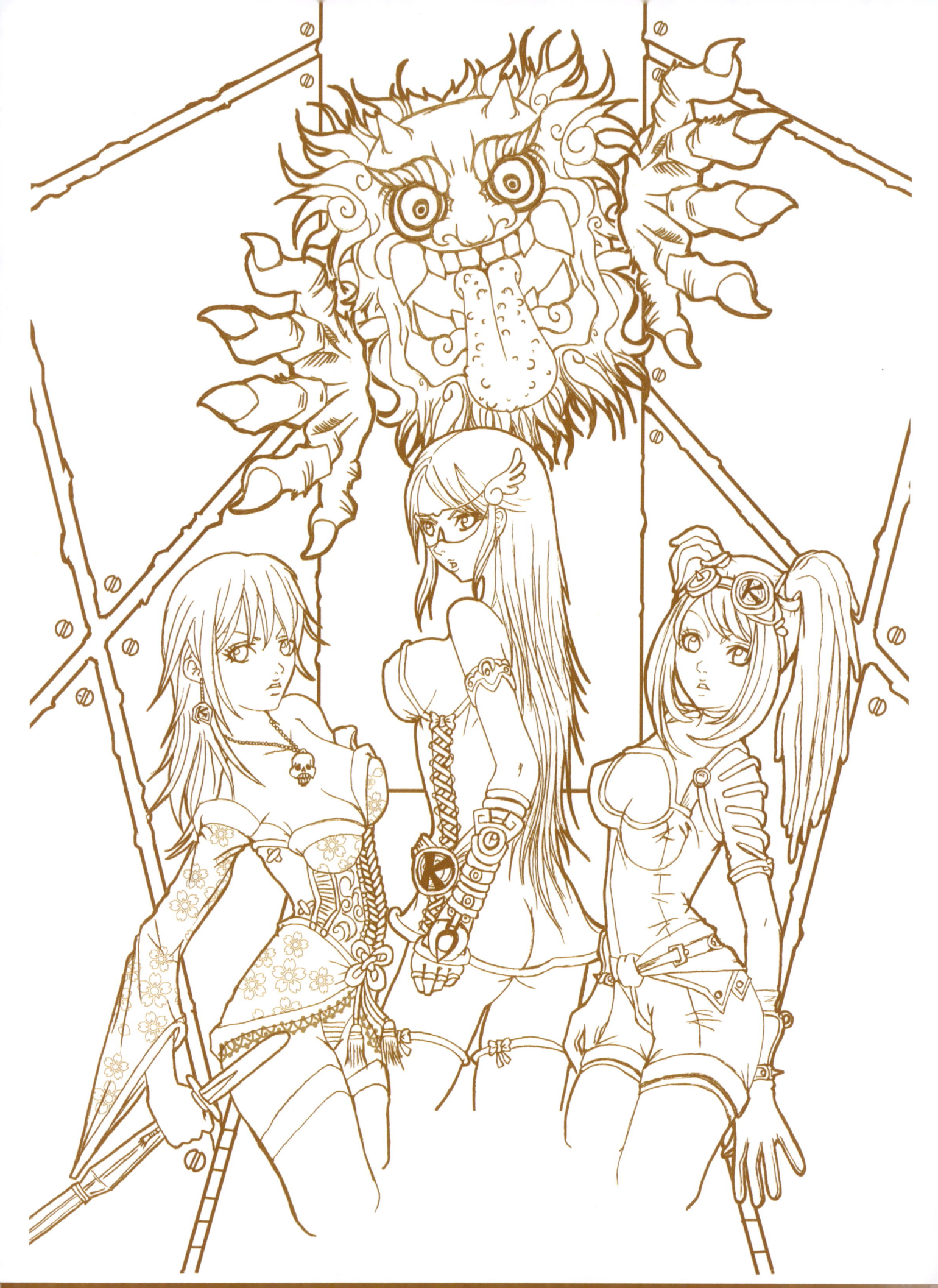

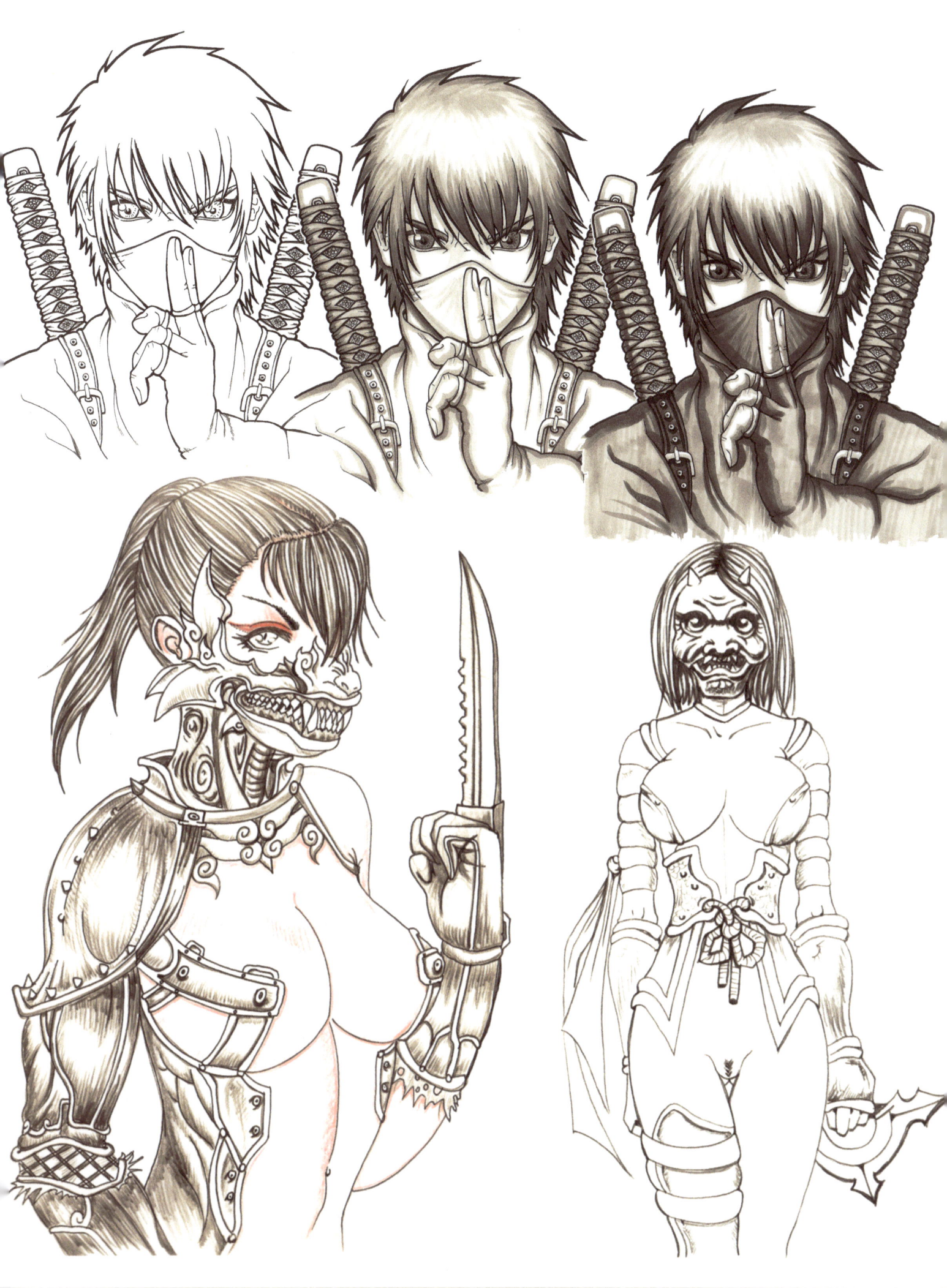

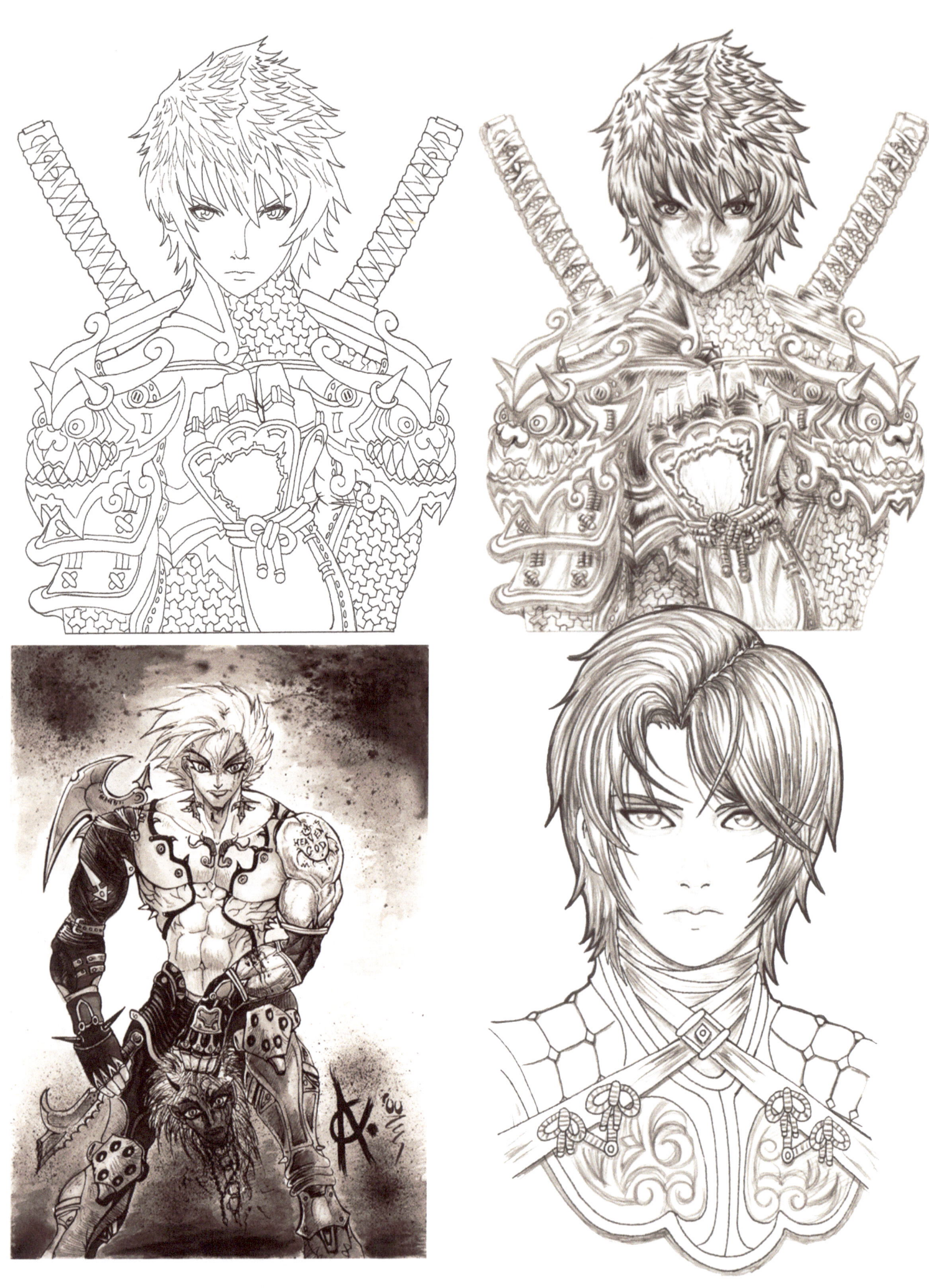

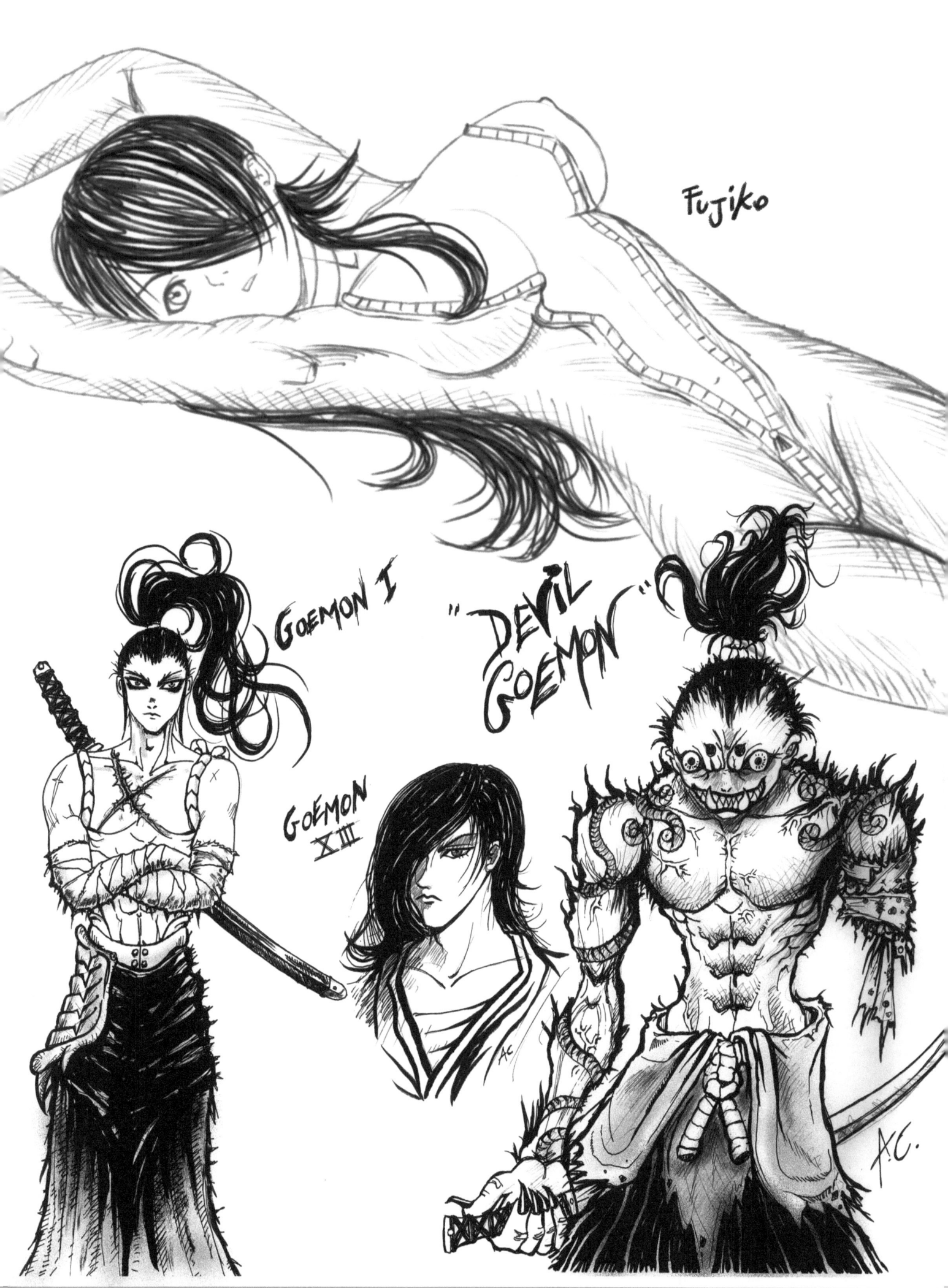

FUJIKO

GOEMON I

"DEVIL GOEMON"

GOEMON XIII

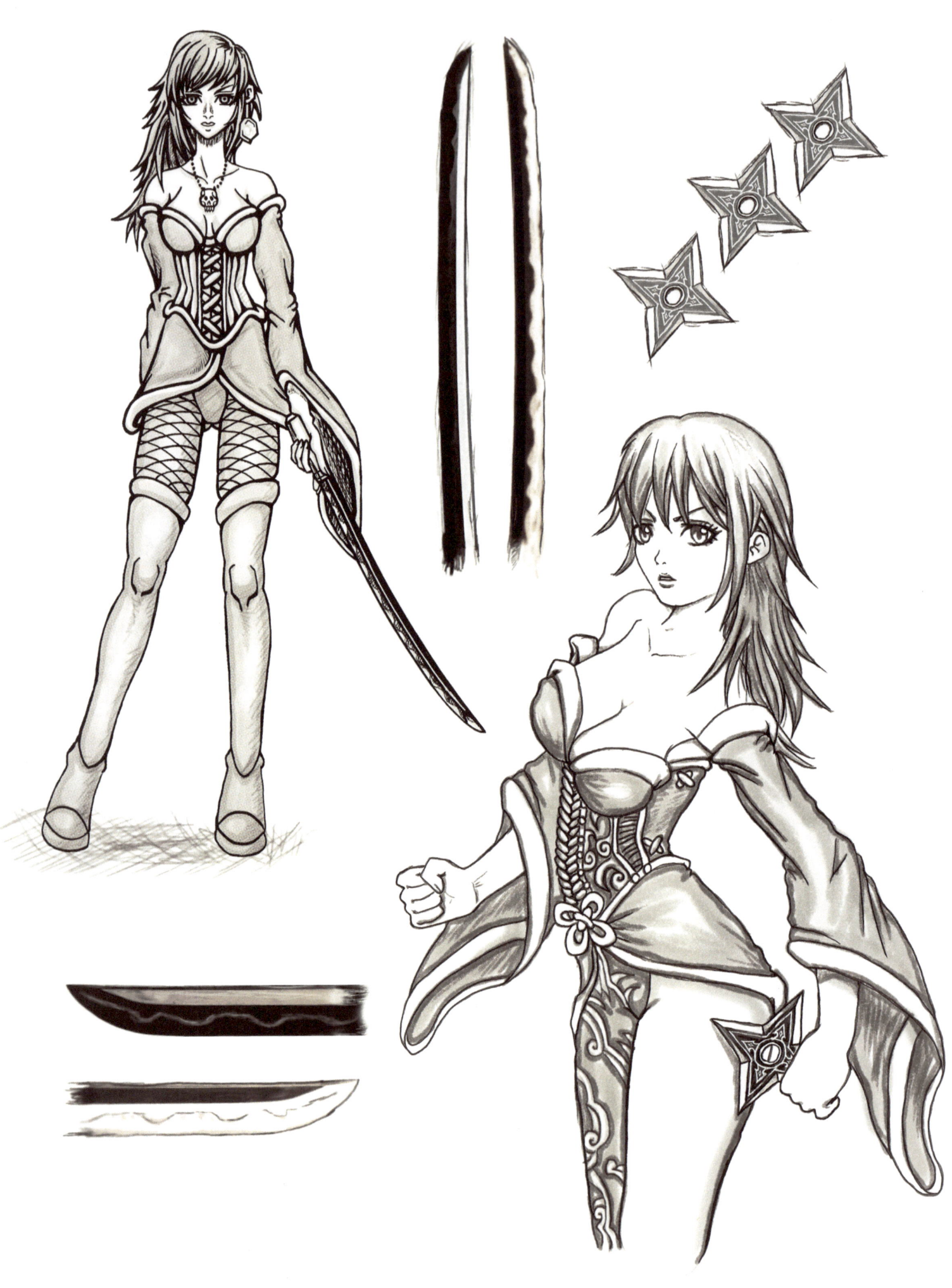

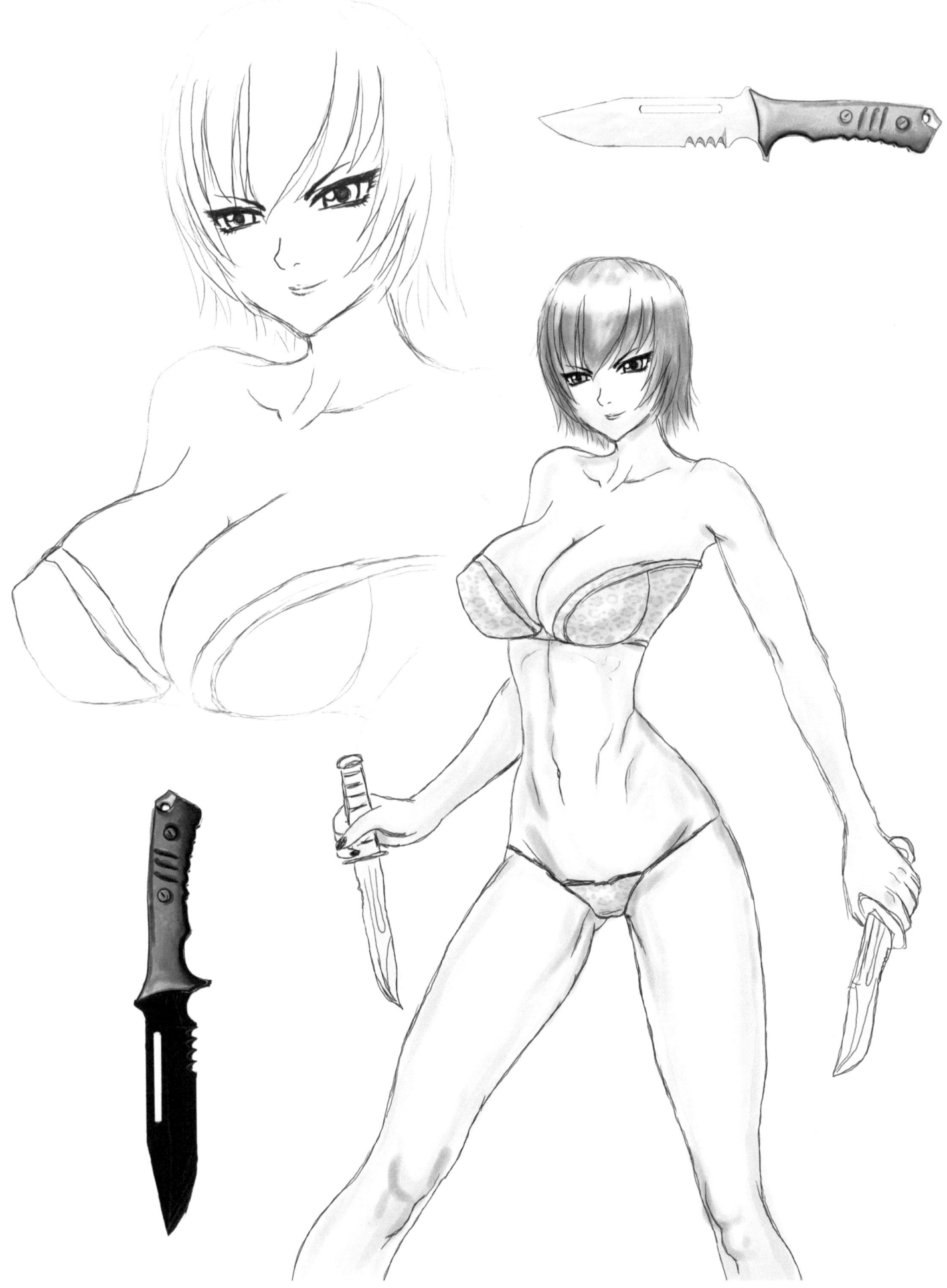

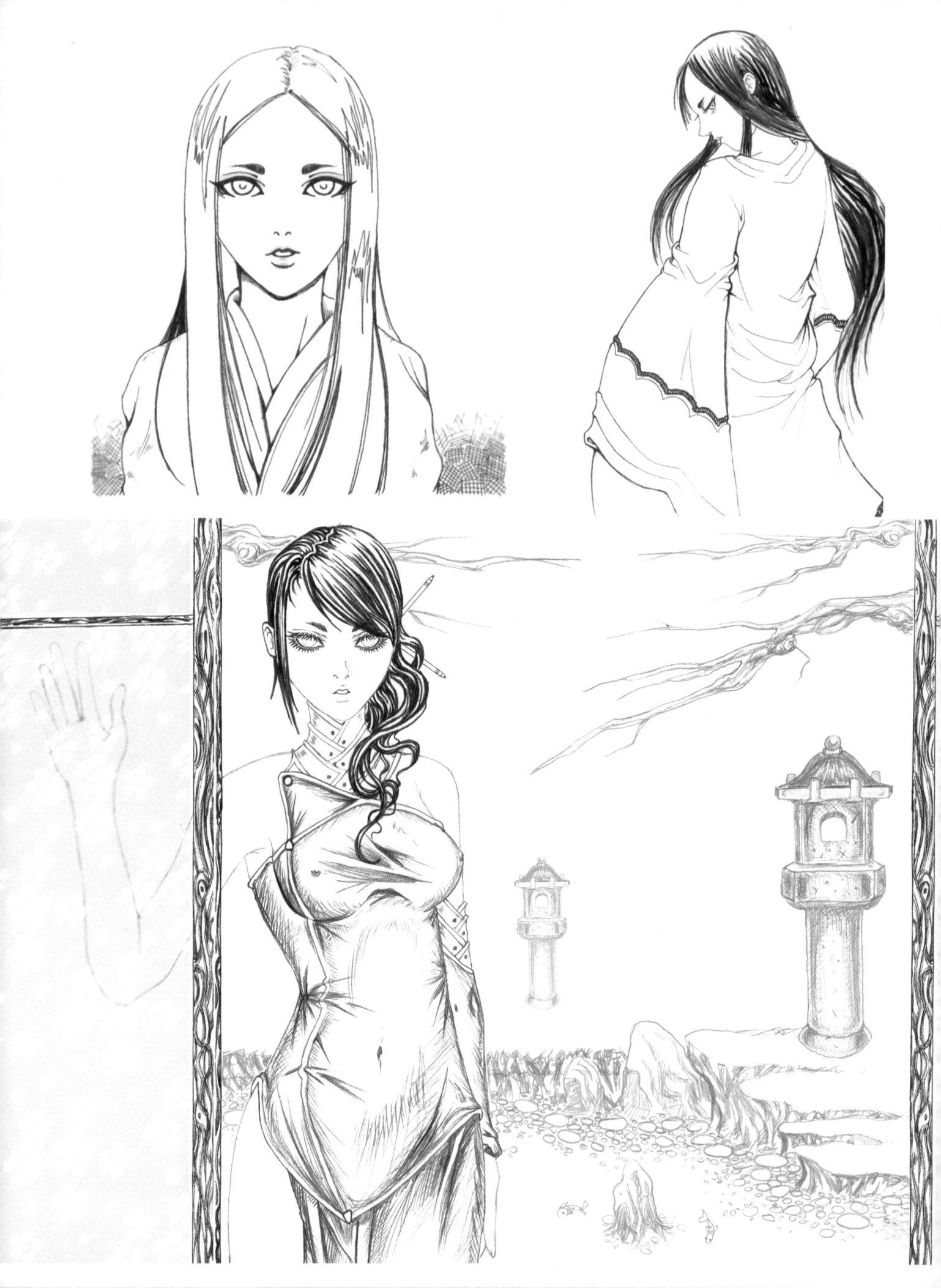

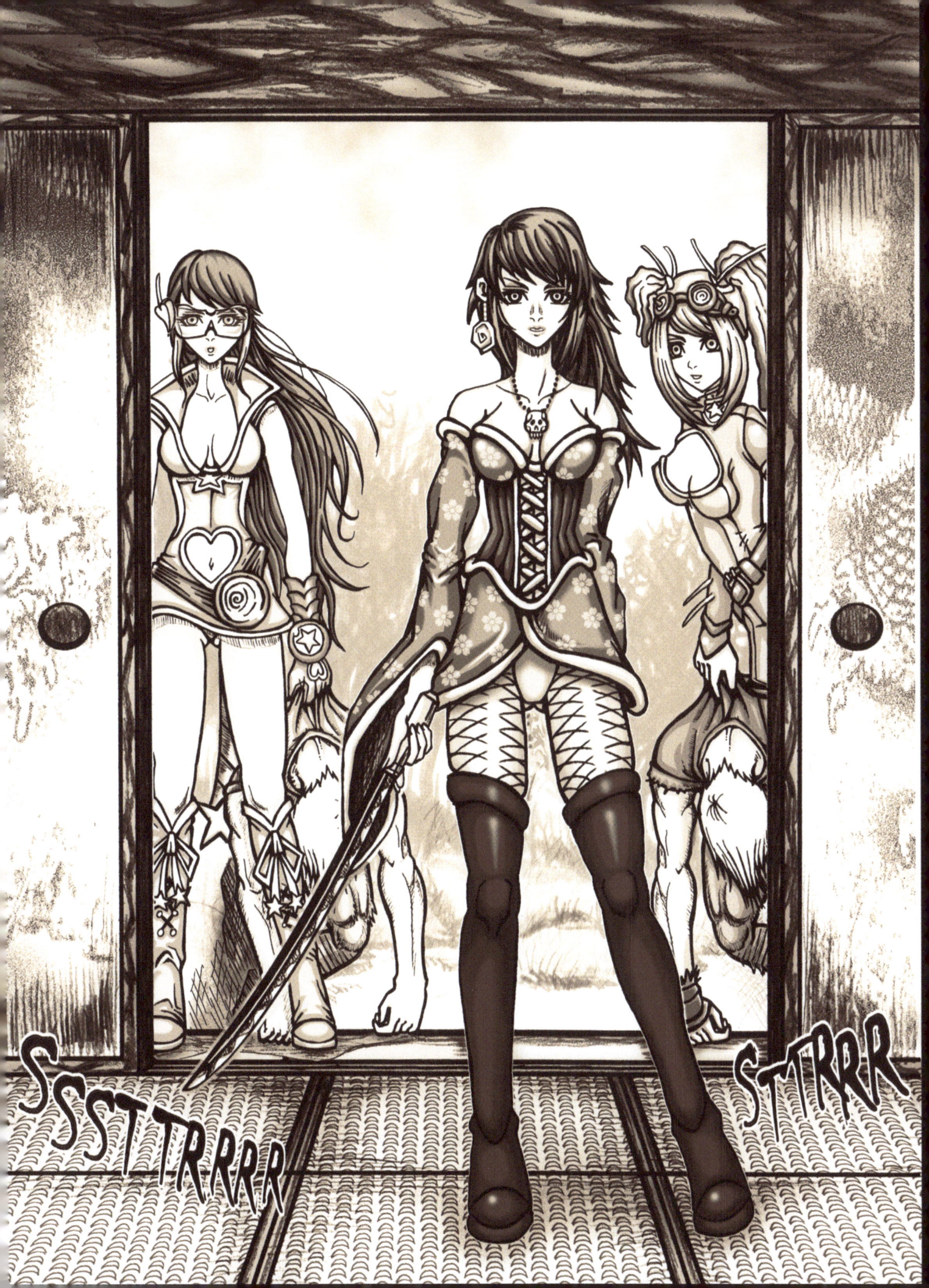

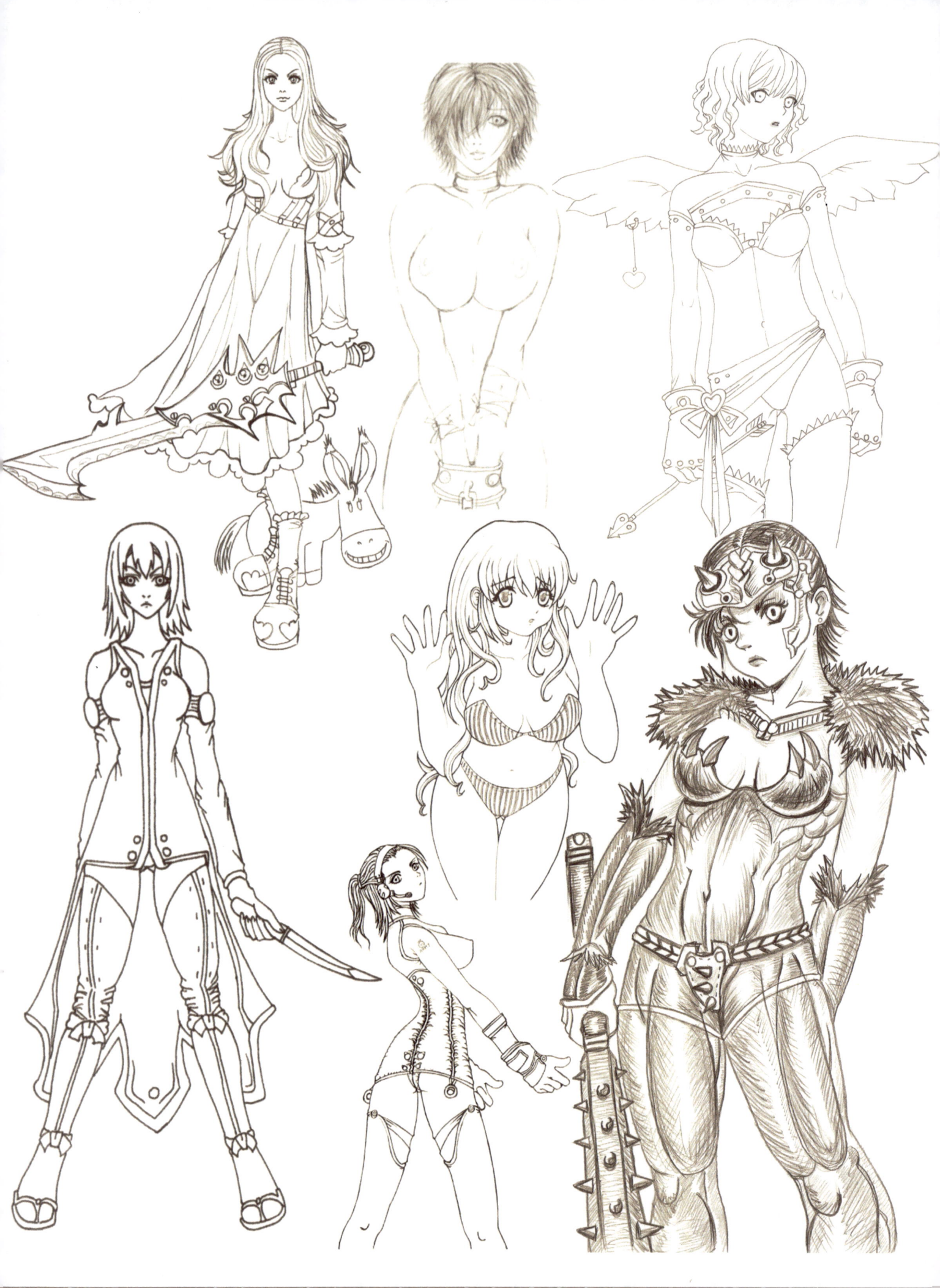

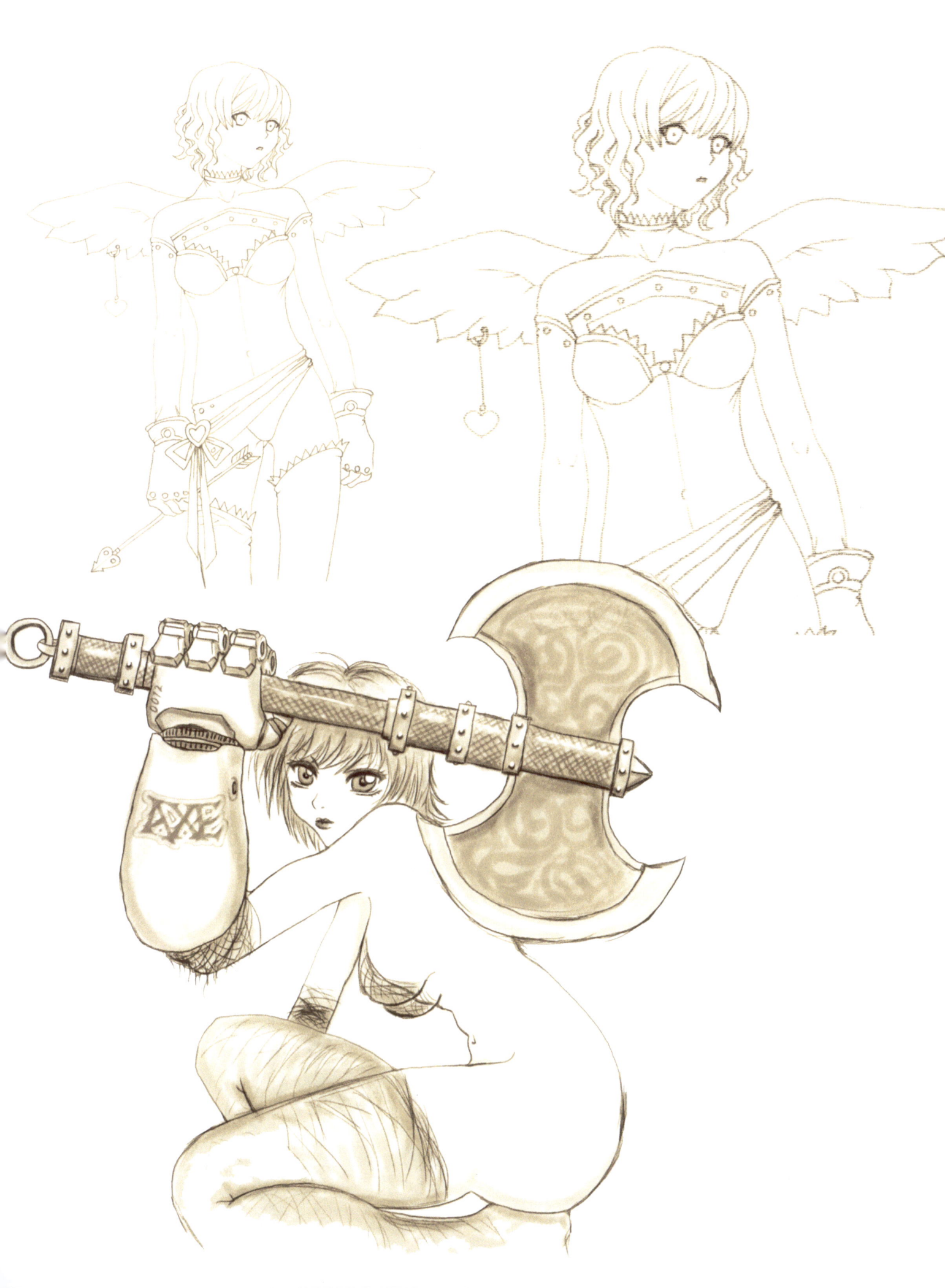

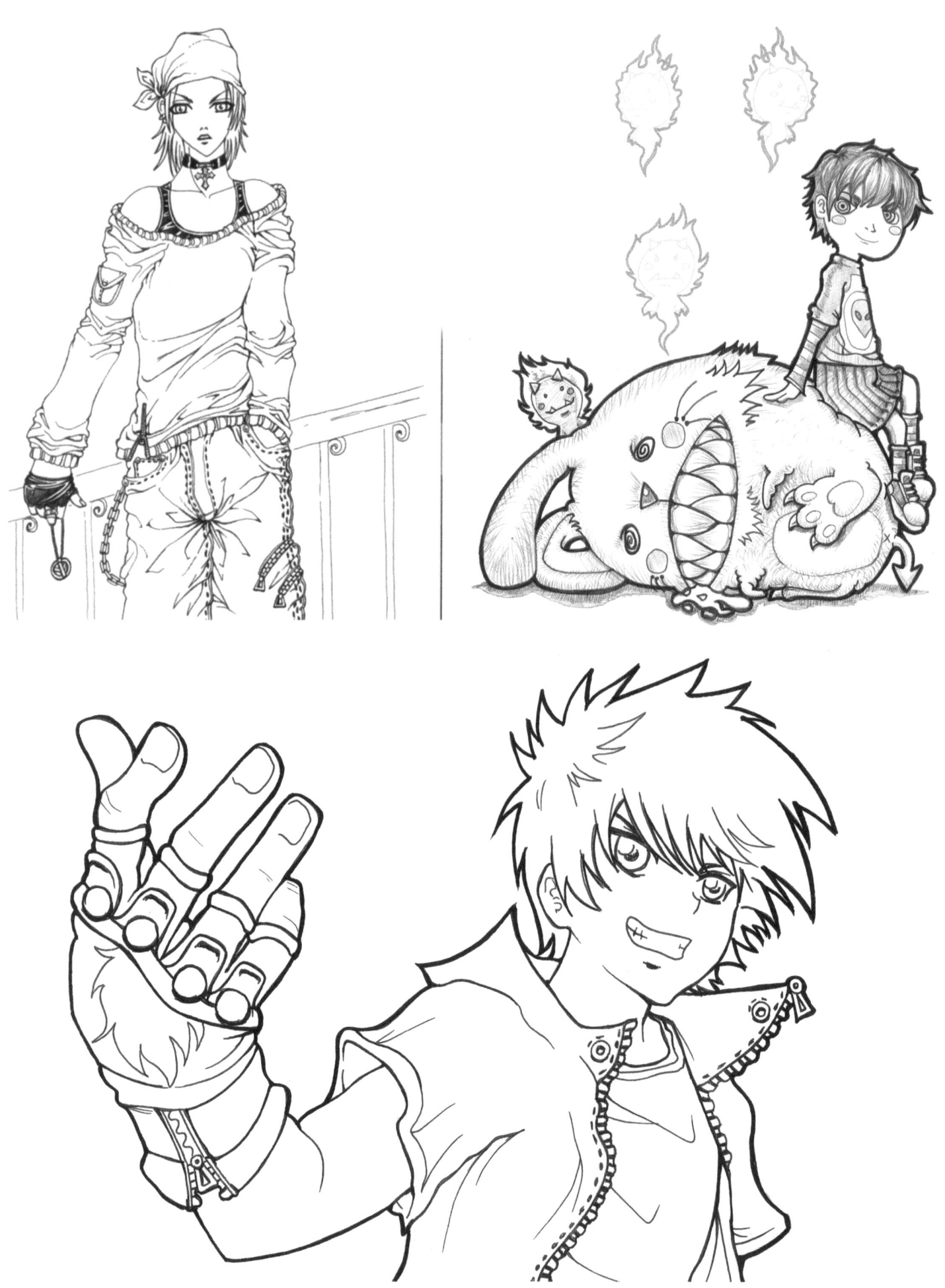

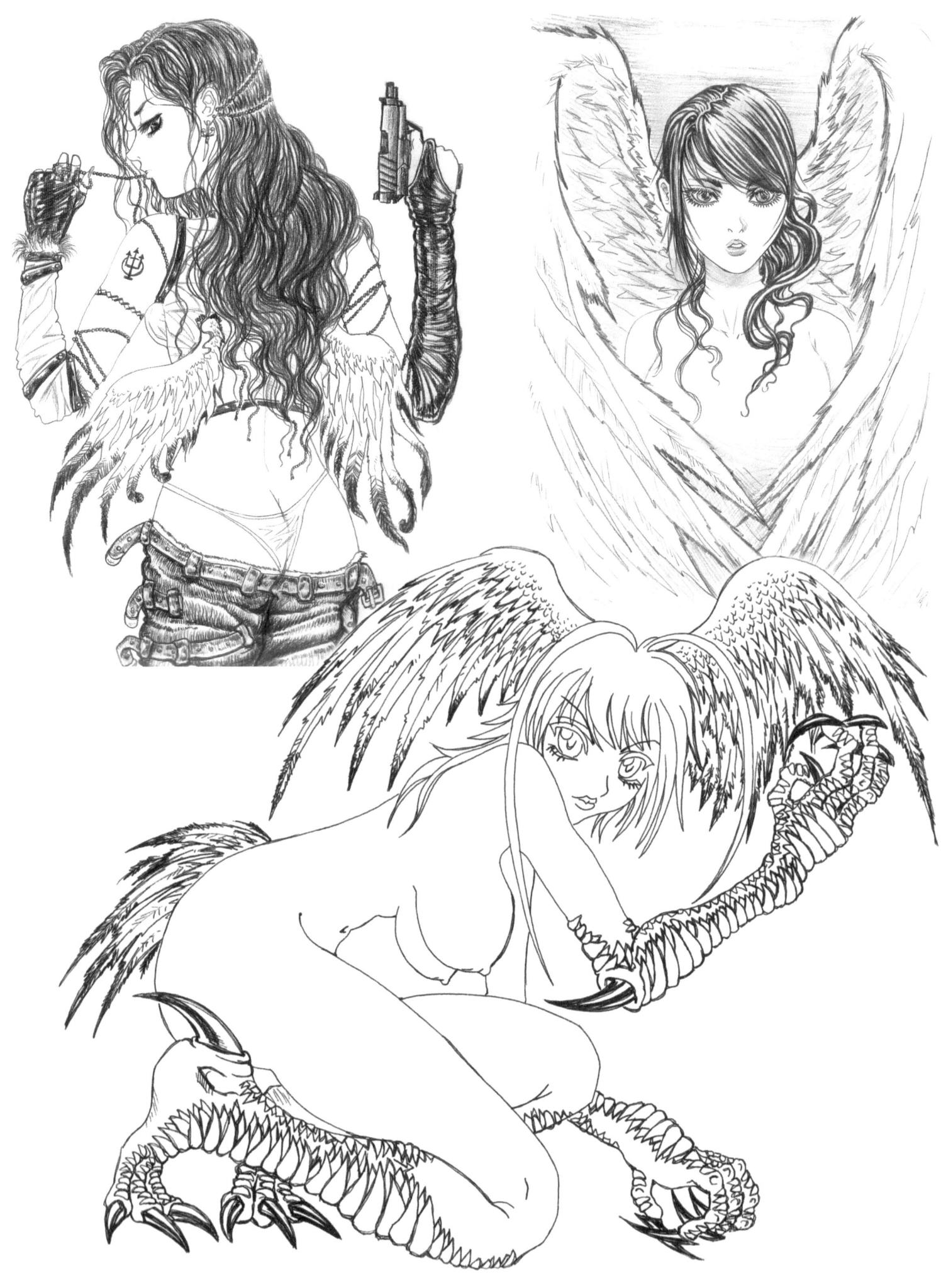

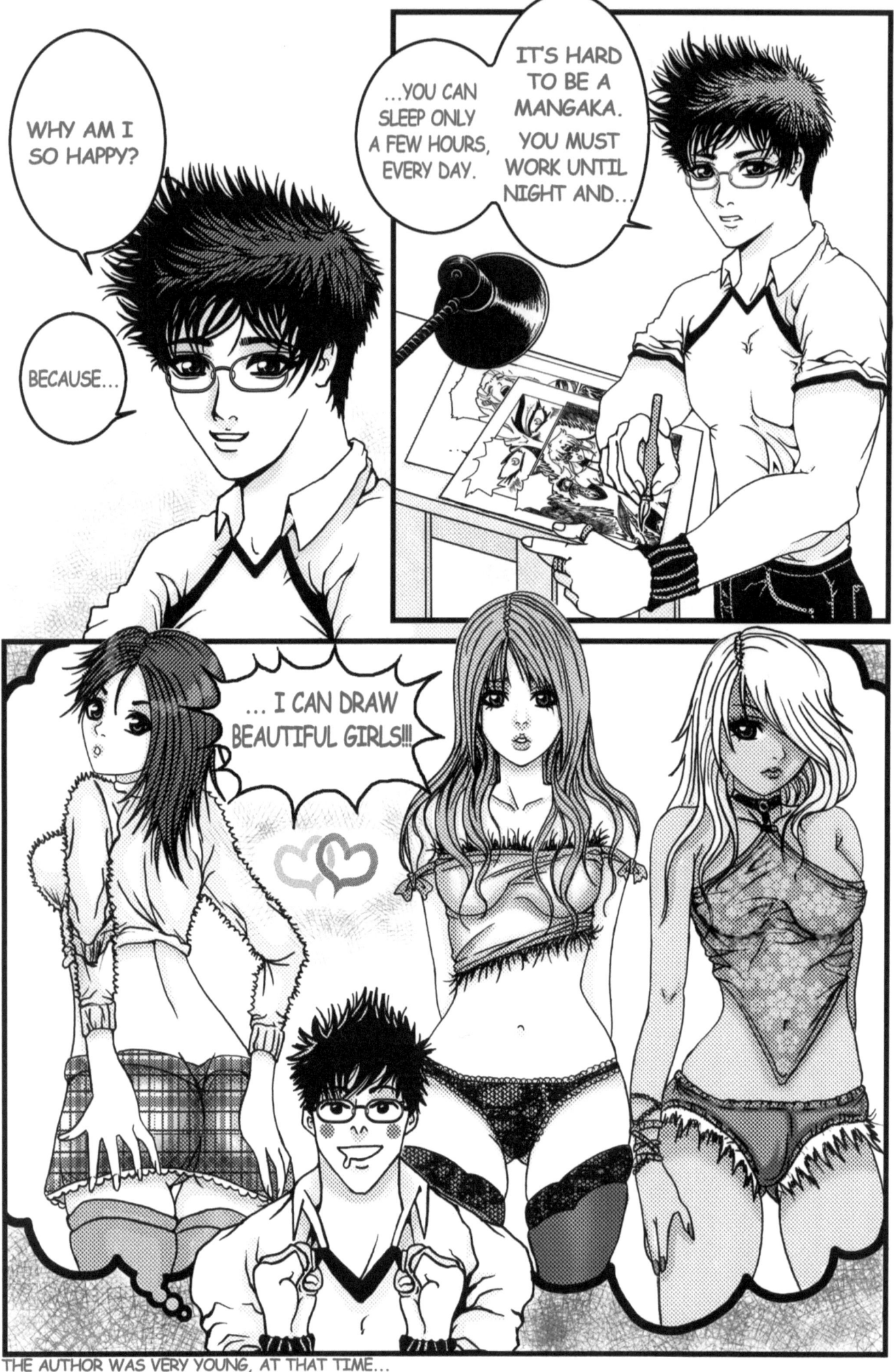

THE AUTHOR WAS VERY YOUNG, AT THAT TIME...